This ship is just like a moving palace it is about two city blocks long, and every inch of it is beautiful the lounges and ba... ... ... perfect. my stateroom is on the outside with two port holes far above the water so can have them open. a moving picture with

LETTERS FROM LUCIA

LETTERS FROM LUCIA

A YOUNG WOMAN'S TRAVELS TO ENGLAND AS WWII LOOMS

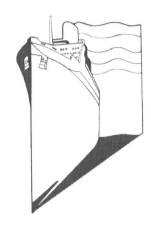

Kathleen M. Cargill

BEEKEEPERS PRESS

DULUTH, MINNESOTA

LETTERS FROM LUCIA

A Young Woman's Travels to England as WWII Looms

ISBN 978-0-9890478-5-2

Printed and bound in the United States of America
Book layout and design by Marlene Wisuri
Dovetailed Press LLC

Cover photo and interior photographs are from the
collection of Kathleen M. Cargill

BEEKEEPERS PRESS

DULUTH, MINNESOTA

TABLE OF CONTENTS

PREFACE

My life was filled with stories about my maternal aunt, Lucia S. Payton. I knew her when I was a child, but the last time I spoke to her I was about age eighteen and she was about age fifty-two. Stories or comments about Lucia were a part of virtually every holiday or life event in the Payton clan. Lucia's life experiences were dismissed by many of her siblings, even as events happened, and that negativity was passed on to the next generation. As I started the genealogical study of my father's family and then my mother's, I gained a perspective from documents staring at me in black and white. Documents often belie the tales or legends told about family members and this was surely the case for Aunt Lucia. I refused to believe that any one person could be so dreadful. I set about to discover for myself what kind of a woman Lucia Payton was and who she became. I determined to make her life more transparent than the sum of the negative assumptions she received. Welcome to my journey of getting to know my Aunt Lucia.

LUCIA PEYTON TO EUROPE

Miss Lucia Peyton of Wayzata will sail May 23 from New York on the Nieuw Amsterdam for a three months' vacation in England. She will visit relatives in Bishopsworth, Dundry and Stratford-on-Avon and will spend some time in London and Scotland. She will return to Minneapolis late in August.

Article as it appeared in the *Minneapolis Star Tribune* on Sunday, May 14, 1939, and referenced in her Letter 2 on May 22, 1939, just before she boarded the ship. Her last name is misspelled.

...While they were taking pictures of me a lady dashed up & said "are you from Mpls," then asked to take my picture for the Journal, did you see it?

Lucia Sydney Payton (nee Lucy Stellabelle Payton, born in November 1911), my maternal aunt, was the fifth daughter and sixth child of thirteen born to Herbert Edwin Payton and Eugenie Ann Hollis Payton. She was already an outdoors woman and a seasoned traveler within the United States by the time she decided to set sail for England to visit her father's relatives. Her earlier travels and those after WWII are described briefly at the close of this story which focusses on her trip from May 21 through August 11, 1939.

After acquiring Aunt Lucia's scrapbooks and photo albums, I transcribed her original 1939 letters during the summer 2016. The dated letters were slipped inside her personal photo album chronicling her trip. In the album, she glued photos of several people she sailed with or visited in England, and of her sightseeing trips in England. The photo captions were very brief – a word or two. By chance one photo fell off its page, and I discovered much more information written on the back. On a hunch, I carefully pried several other 2 x 3 inch photos from the pages; it was easy as the decades-old glue had dried out. Writings on the back revealed details about her trip that Aunt Lucia had not recorded in her letters.

She sailed tourist class aboard the *S.S. Nieuw Amsterdam* (a luxury cruise liner in the Holland-America Line). She wrote her letters as events unfolded aboard the train from Minneapolis to New York, on the ship, and while visiting in England. They were mailed from England to Dr. Wellington William "Duke" Rieke and his wife Merle Ione Erckenbrack Rieke, her close friends living in Wayzata, Minnesota (population under 1500 in 1939). Her trip was one that thousands of people made that year, either for pleasure or to escape political extremism. Everyday life went on within a darkening backdrop.

Every attempt has been made to keep the punctuation as she used it in the letters. Lucia's handwriting was very good. However, she often truncated or omitted punctuation, giving the reader a sense that she was excited and in a rush to write down her thoughts. She did not write letters on the return trip, nor is there an existing journal, but she did have a few photos from the return journey.

Editorial comments follow each letter and are interwoven to set her travels within their historical context. The *Afterwords I* and *II* are devoted to vignettes about many of her fellow passengers traveling to England in May and those returning to the United States in August.

England's Prelude to World War II

The reasons that World War II occurred are myriad and cannot be gone into detail in this book. There are hundreds, if not thousands, of historical references that discuss these reasons; I refer my readers to those. In short, however, some reasons are: the situation in Germany after World War I caused great economic stress; Japan invaded Manchuria in 1931 to secure greater land for their growing population; Japan was also interested in British oil and rubber territories in Malay and Burma as they had no secure source for these products; the Horn of Africa (Ethiopia) was invaded by the Fascist dictator Benito Mussolini in 1935 as was his invasion of Somalia in 1923 and his helping the nationalists in the Spanish Civil War (1936-1939); and Hitler had moved across Europe in his quest to build an empire. By the summer of 1939, it was apparent to the world that war was coming and would pit Japan, Germany, and Italy against England, the British Empire, the United States of America, Russia, and China.

Once war became inevitable, the British government added to their preparations in December 1938. For example, historically important information is tabulated on the *1939 Register*, a brief snapshot of forty-one million British citizens collected on September 29. The nation knew it had to issue national identity cards, plan for a wide-scale mobilization of its population, plan for the eventual introduction of rationing, and plan for possible evacuations from large cities, particularly the coastal port cities.

The nation's most recent census was almost a decade old, so more up-to-date statistics were needed. Preparations had begun for the 1941 UK Census, so the government capitalized on this to take a register of the civilian population. It issued Identity Cards immediately afterwards and used them until 1952. The Government constantly updated the *1939 Register* over time to include changes of address or deaths. When rationing was introduced in 1941, the Government planned it with information from the *1939 Register*. The British government needed to know the skills and occupations it could call upon to meet the needs of its people during a war. The Register required British citizens to give precise data about their occupation, adding details of the trade, manufacture or branch of profession. I researched both the transcription of the data and reviewed each image of the original entry.

The Payton clan was certainly among those enumerated. Information about those whom Lucia visited is included to lend to the historical context. I searched the *1939 Register* for Payton ancestors and those who married into the Payton family line. I used surnames for the most part, with good results. I learned the name of the person, name of the second person (most often, the wife), marital status, address, full date of birth, occupation, and gender. The Payton family comes from a long line of stone workers, bricklayers, heavy laborers, heavy metal workers, road laborers, carpenters, mason, and farmers. The Paytons were parish clerks involved in St. Michael's the Archangel Church back to at least 1568, according to the original hand-written church records I used to trace the Payton family's participation in the church.

Lucia's trip, set in a context of global events, reflects an isolationist attitude held by both American government officials and many within the American public. Germany had annexed Austria in March 1938; the *Anschlus* occurred March 10 to March 14. Several events which occurred in the months just prior to her voyage include: January 30, 1939, Adolf Hitler called for the extermination of Jews; February 25, 1939, England erected the first Anderson bomb shelter in Islington Garden; March 14, 1939, Hitler occupied Czechoslovakia and the Nazi *Wehrmacht* annexed the Sudentenland; May 22, 1939, Hitler and Italy's leader Benito Mussolini signed a "Pact of Steel"; and on March 31 Hitler signed a Treaty of Friendship with General Francisco Franco, the dictator of Spain.

England prepared for war throughout 1939, with preparations becoming more intense during the summer months immediately preceding Hitler's invasion of Poland on September 1. Given knowledge of these events, it is remarkable that anyone would plan a pleasure cruise during the summer of 1939. There had to have been a sense of urgency or anxiety among some of the passengers, particularly those on the return voyage in August 1939.

During that Minnesota spring, twenty-seven year old Lucia Sydney Payton, prepared for a ten-week summer visit to her Payton family relatives in England (her father's brothers and sisters). She traveled by train from Minneapolis through Chicago and on to New York City. From there she sailed to Plymouth, England, from May 22, 1939, through May 29, 1939. The passenger list stated she was headed to Bristol Oak Tree Farm, Bishopsworth and Dundry, Somerset County, in southwest England. She was a U.S. citizen. Her occupation was "Teloperator" and she was passenger #180. Master of the ship was Abraham Filippo. I found this information on the *UK, Incoming Passenger List, 1878-1960 for Lucia Payton, "Names and Descriptions of Alien Passengers."*

Brief mention needs to be made about Aunt Lucia's background and how she created a way to experience such a fabulous trip just at the end of the Depression. It is important to note that until this voyage, none of Lucia's siblings had ever traveled outside the United States, except her eldest brother, George Herbert Payton, who served in the U. S. Navy and was stationed in Australia between World War I and World War II.

Her parents, the young widow, Eugenie Ann Hollis Hinson, Hamilton, Bermuda, and British Army Sergeant Herbert Edwin Payton, Somerset, England, were married in Bermuda on September 7, 1903. Four days later, Eugenie, still using her first husband's last name, sailed to the United States aboard the *S.S. Trinidad*, to join her mother, Susan Catherine Smith Hollis, widow of John Nelson Hollis. The latter woman had immigrated to the United States in July 1902, with her two youngest children, Evelyn Kenneth Hollis and Richard Arthur Hollis. Eugenie's eldest living sister, Florence Isabelle Hollis Pogue, already lived in Minnetonka, Minnesota, and was married to Jasper Marcus Pogue, an Itasca County, Minnesota, native.

On or about March 28, 1904, Herbert Payton, who had joined the British Army at age eighteen, and served in Bermuda as a guard of prisoners of war from the Second Boer War, deserted to join his new wife in Minnesota. He did not serve the last five years of a twelve-year commitment in the Reserves.

Lucia's upbringing in Wayzata, Minnesota, was impoverished. Although her father was a mason/plasterer and had a garden and a cow, his earnings were insufficient to adequately feed and clothe thirteen children born between 1905 and 1925. My mother, one of Lucia's elder sisters, and other maternal aunts often spoke of the material and nutritional deprivation within the household as they grew up. Lucia's mother often worked as a laundress or a nanny in the homes of wealthy people in the Lake Minnetonka area until she was in her late 70s. Also, it was not uncommon for some of Lucia's elder sisters to serve while they were teenagers as housekeepers for "the rich people."

Lucia Sydney Payton was an inveterate traveler. She often went with female friends or couples. In 1930, at the age of eighteen, Lucia lived briefly with one elder sister, Florence Isabelle Payton Cargill and her brother-in-law John Charles Cargill (my parents) in Mifflintown, Pennsylvania. Neither Lucia nor Florence had completed high school. It is not known exactly what year the three arrived in Pennsylvania, but it may have been as early as 1929. Florence was still recovering from the loss of her first child on May 11, 1928, just twelve months after her marriage on June 1, 1927. Florence wanted someone she knew to be with her in Pennsylvania. The *1930 US Census* indicated that John Cargill was a store manager, and it is believed the store was owned by his ailing adoptive father, John Maurice Cargill and his wife, Sarah Elizabeth Jamison Cargill.

Lucia was back in Wayzata, Minnesota by fall 1932, enrolled in high school. She moved out on her own after graduating high school in 1933. Her graduation from high school came when she was twenty-one years and eight months old as depicted in Lucia's personal 1930s annotated photo album and her graduation photo. The group graduation photo on page 49 is labeled *Wayzata High School Senior Class 1932-1933*. Later, she wore a lovely long white lace dress to be photographed at Wayzata Beach that June to celebrate the event. Clearly, she was proud of this moment in her life.

Sometime after 1933 and before 1939, she changed her name from Lucy Stellabelle Payton to Lucia Sydney Payton, a clear step in re-inventing herself. Nine of the Payton siblings were named for an ancestor primarily in their father's lineage back to the 16th Century; a few from their mother's lineage in Bermuda. This was a common practice for the clan, and sometimes a challenge in reckoning kinship. Aunt Lucia, as a child named Lucy, likely was named after her father's younger sister, Lucy Ellen Payton.

On a telephone operator's salary, she made her own way, and afforded this extravagant trip while her five elder siblings married and struggled to make ends meet during the Depression. She and her younger siblings married after 1940. Lucia's 1939 trip and subsequent travel in the United States, Bermuda, and France, was wonderful for her, but it left a life-long bitter taste in the mouths of many of her siblings.

At this point in this very personal research, I realized I wanted to tell the story of a woman who set herself apart from her family, eschewing participation in family celebrations with her siblings, including not attending (or perhaps briefly attending) the funerals of her parents. However, she maintained contact with the clan's youngest brother, William Arthur Payton, throughout her life. She did keep in touch with some of her nieces who lived in Wayzata and France and established friendships with local Wayzata residents who had cross-over relationships with her parents and her siblings. Wayzata was a very small town, populated by families who had known each other for generations. Lucia's activities in the Wayzata area often were a focus for conversation among her siblings throughout her life. Her siblings expressed envy and criticism in the often-asked question "Who does she think she is?" I knew all of this from family conversations and my own observations. I wanted to know more about a woman who stepped away from her natal family, and instead reached out to her uncles, aunts, and cousins who lived an ocean away.

CRUISING ABOARD THE SS NIEUW AMSTERDAM

Lucia on the deck of the SS Nieuw Amsterdam.

In 1939, Lucia's cruise included fellow passengers who created an upper class socio-cultural context in which Lucia was immersed on both long voyages. Aunt Lucia would have been very cognizant of the differences between her own upbringing and that of the other passengers. She would have recognized that some passengers traveled with their staff, such as maids, valets, and governesses. Their servants represented many ethnic groups including African Americans ("Negroes"), Portuguese, Irish, Scottish, and Swedish. The *Afterwords I* and *II* contain vignettes of many passengers from both voyages of Lucia's journey. I included these because the passengers and crew members played a part in Lucia's first exciting international experience.

In addition, Lucia's outdoorswoman activities from 1930 to spring, 1939, are illustrated briefly after the letters she wrote to provide a more complete picture of this adventurous woman.

Letter 1 Monday Morning (likely May 21, 1939)

Dearest Merle & Duke,

I'm writing on the train so that I can tell you things as we go. The most impressive thing so far is the difference between the Hiawatha & the Pa. RR. After that smooth ride to Chicago this is like riding a rheumatic plow horse, when the train stops, your head almost snaps off, when the train starts, you almost bite your tongue.

We are just coming into Pittsburgh. It's six in the morning & gloomy as a morgue it's been raining there.

Here is where the beauty begins. We are starting our climb up the mountains & they are all around us as far as we can see. The way this old train is puffing I guess we will have to get out & push. The river that runs at the foot of the mt is red as brick it must be from the iron in the h2o.

My lord you should see the pile of human flesh that just got on & followed, of course, by a puny mouse of a man, she must be two hundred years old – it would take that long to get so much.

Was all thrilled a few minutes ago – thought a gangster sat beside me – he looked just like Ed. G. Robinson but when he spoke it was sort of the Grant Smith type of voice – so –

We are going up such a steep grade that the houses look like they are built on the slant & chickens have one short leg – My ears hurt from the altitude & I believe a nose bleed is coming on – we seem to be going straight up now & the train is hardly moving. The tree tops look a hundred miles below, yet we still have more to go – hope the old boy knows when he hits the top.

We are going around the famous horse shoe curve at Altoona now, I'm so excited everyone is trying to show me places of interest at once.

After two hours in the mt we decide to go down the other side & have been coasting for some time & if he goes one mile faster, I'll drag my feet so help me.

Well we got here but now the huge rocks are jutting over our heads at a very precarious angle. I breath {sic} a sigh of relief when we get safely under.

The fat lady is warming up & how I hoped for a cool day.

Philadelphia is a funny old city everything looks alike. The architect evidently had no imagination.

Here I am at the hotel in a much too expensive room on the eighteenth floor it's very beautiful done in green & cream & I keep rushing to the window to see the skyline & it surely scares me the darn place is too big & feel like that worm you found Sunday.

I'm going to dash out now & eat then go to bed – I don't need to tell you how I wish you were both here in fact I don't dare think.

Oceans of love   Lucia

Comments about Letter I

Lucia would have taken the morning or afternoon Hiawatha train or the Milwaukee Road as these were the two fastest trains of the day. They were also the most convenient in that they originated in Minneapolis and Chicago and were not through trains from elsewhere like the Great Northern Empire Builder was, according to Ken Buehler, Executive Director of the Lake Superior Railroad Museum in Duluth, Minnesota. He added that the morning and afternoon "Hi's" were more popular because they were direct; the morning Hiawatha left Minneapolis at 7:50 AM and arrived in Chicago's Union Station at 2:40 PM. The Milwaukee Road connected with the Pennsylvania Railroad at Union Station.

On the Pennsylvania, Lucia would have taken the Broadway Limited leaving Union Station at 3:30 PM daily, and arriving in North Philadelphia at 7:09 AM, then arrived at New York's Penn Station at 8:30 AM. This was an all First Class train with dining car, café/lounge/observation car and Pullman Sleeping Cars. It appears Aunt Lucia started her journey in luxury! During WWII, over seventeen million military personnel were moved by the Pennsylvania Railroad. The train traveled through the Alleghany Mountains, part of the Appalachian Chain.

The Hollywood movie star she referenced was Edward Goldenberg Robinson, who famously portrayed Little Caesar, a fictional hood. Grant Smith was another movie star of the 1930s.

Horse Shoe Curve, outside Altoona, Pennsylvania, is at the base of the Allegheny Mountains, and opened February 15, 1854. It greatly facilitated transportation from Philadelphia to Pittsburgh. Horse Shoe Curve was on a list of twelve key industrial sites targeted by Nazi saboteurs who were captured at two sites off the coast of the United States in June 1942. The Pennsylvania Railroad was headquartered in Philadelphia.

Although she does not name the hotel, she later used stationery labeled *Hotel McAlpin, New York*. When it opened in 1912 it was the largest hotel in the world. The *New York Times* commented that it was so tall at 25 floors that it "seems isolated from other buildings." With a staff of 1,500 it could accommodate 2,500 guests. The 1500-room McAlpin

Hotel was designed by Frank Mills Andrews (1867-1948), one of the most prolific early 19th C architects and developers. Room rates per day varied: about $4.00 secured a single room with a bath, or a set of rooms with parlor, bedroom, and bath cost $15. Lucia's was a single room with a bath so she paid from $3.85 to $6.50.

The 1939 New York World's Fair opened April 30 and ran for two years, which means there was a lot of activity in New York City when Aunt Lucia was there. The Fair, held in Queens, included participation by states and foreign countries, big and small businesses, cultural, scientific and religious bodies. The focus was on the future, with a slogan of *Dawn of a New Day*. Its theme of *The World Tomorrow* shifted in 1940 to *For Peace and Freedom*.

The cost of travel

Aunt Lucia was able to afford this luxurious trip because she worked as an operator at the telephone exchange for the Northwestern Bell Telephone Company from at least 1937 to 1940. There is a photo of her at work later in the story on page 51.

1940 US Census indicates she earned $900/year and worked 40 hours/week for about $17.30 weekly. Trends in occupations outside the home for women included that of telephone operator because of the rapid development in communications nationwide. Women were vastly unemployed during the Depression, but by the late 1930s, the economy improved and jobs opened up.

By 1930 there were 235,259 women employed as telephone operators; by 1937 94% of telephone operators were women for a total of 281,204. By comparison other "white collar" workers earned a bit more annually: teachers earned between $999 and $3,300, librarians earned $1,110 and $1,950.50, and clerical workers earned between $1,253 and $1,881 in 1937.

The cost of her cruise on Holland-American Line is likely similar to the cost of one on the French Line, which also offered cabin (first class), tourist, and third class accommodations. In 1933, at the height of the Great Depression, a cabin class fare was $159, inclusive of meals and all activities. Lucia traveled Tourist Class, double occupancy, on both legs of the voyage. Her fare was computed for the High Season, May 13 to September 30, 1939, at $144 each way. Her accommodations would have been luxurious for the time.

On May 23, 1939, *Reichsfurer* Adolf Hitler auspiciously announced he wanted to move into Poland.

Lucia S. Payton on her first day aboard *SS Nieuw Amsterdam.* She is very stylishly dressed with hat, gloves, purse and probably wearing a navy blue dress.

Letter 2 (Tuesday, May 22, 1939 written on ship's stationery)
First Day at Sea

Dear Merle & Duke,

No mail leaves the boat so I will write everyday & mail all of it in England.

Dorothy Peterson & her friend took me out to breakfast & came to the boat with me. While they were taking pictures of me a lady dashed up & said "are you from Mpls," then asked to take my picture for the Journal, did you see it?

The ship is just like a moving palace, it is about two city blocks long, and every inch of it is beautiful, the lounges and bar room which is also a dance hall are perfect – my stateroom is on the outside with two port holes far above the water so I can have them open. A moving picture with sound also.

The crew is entirely dutch {sic}, and I'm having a time because most of the passengers don't speak English either.

Found myself a forty year old (or there about) play boy who just got back from South America & will now tour Europe, he is a good entertainer – plays all the games with me & shows me all around the boat, he will do until I meet some younger men.

The dining room is gorgeous & we are all given a permanent place for meals. I'm to sit at a large table to get better acquainted so will write more of that later.

I have a woman doctor from Austria in my cabin, she doesn't speak English very well but we get along for I'm on deck mostly.

It was foggy when we left New York so I didn't see the statue {of Liberty} – it has been that way all day too. The water is a bit rough, not bad though the vibration of the ship makes me dizzy when I stop long enough to notice, you get used to that they tell me.

We go to dinner in about ten minutes after that is a movie – what an exciting day.

Had a wonderful dinner with a menu just like the hotel, then saw Heart of the North in sound. Ran down here again to tell you I must dress for I'm going dancing in the bar, oh boy!

2nd Day (Wednesday, May 23, aboard the ship)

Good morning folks, slept like a log in fact didn't wake until ten then had to rush for breakfast – by the way they make their toast by frying it in something – not good.

The strangest thing so far is the lack of wash cloths, although the bath towels are large enough to cover Duke – the Austrian says they never use wash cloths in Europe but wash with their hands, she had one fortunately & gave it to me.

It is very choppy this morning but the sun is shining so I'll take pictures – see you later.

Just heard a grand concert & flirted a little with the piano player because he blushes so funny – he is a fellow larger than you Duke with yellow hair & I mean yellow – he speaks only Dutch.

Got myself a deck chair & blanket this morning, sat in the sun about ten minutes when the play boy came to walk me around the deck. Think I'll swim after lunch.

We have a woman on board who thinks she's Mrs. Aster's {sic} plush horse, in fact she told the chief steward, she couldn't get used to eating with us for she always sat at the captain's table – I told the chief she was a sour puss, the name went over the ship like wildfire everyone calls her that now. I asked him if I could trip her, he said, "and how only do it near the rail so she will fall in."

The people at my table are all making their first trip, two old couples & a bride & groom and a little Chinese girl, also another man who is an American underwriter for Lloyds of London.

I'm so thrilled about everything that this trip isn't going to last long enough.

We had caps and balloons besides a grand dinner tonight. I'm sending the menu.

The waiters & stewards are so friendly they say "OK" & "hi" to me now, but it took them a long time to catch on.

The two men who have deck chairs next to mine are Americans, there are only eighty of us on the boat – the younger of the two has a movie camera & has been making pictures of me all morning.

The program I sent tells all we do & I do it all so won't bother to write.

Tonight is a dance again & am I going to make hay –

Lucia seated on her assigned deck chair with blanket.

Comments about Letter 2

I puzzled over the "Dorothy Peterson" she mentioned as having taken her out to breakfast before the boat launched. Since this is a common name, I reasoned that the Riekes, to whom Lucia was writing, would have to know who this was. I consulted with my younger brother, Herb Cargill, who recalled Dorothy Peterson was a friend to our parents, along with her sister, Elvia and their mother. I confirmed that **Dorothy Peterson** was born Dorothy Alethea Horton, one of three children born to Theresa Horton, whom my brother and I called "Nanny Horton." The Horton family lived in Plymouth, Minnesota, and would have been known to other families in the Wayzata area. I have not been able to discover what Dorothy was doing in New York in 1939, nor why she was listed by her own family name in the *1940 US Census*. This person, therefore, remains an "almost-solved" mystery.

According to her description and to the diagrams contained in the *Tourist and Third Class Plan*, found in her photo album, Lucia's cabin was a double-occupancy room and could have been on A, B or C Deck. Each deck contained Cabin Class, Tourist and Third Class rooms and other rooms suitable for small and large gatherings.

There were two hundred seventy-three "alien" passengers (*i.e.*, non-British citizens, including about one hundred sixty-six Americans), according to the *UK, Incoming Passenger List 1878-1960, "Names and Description of ALIEN Passengers."* *Nieuw Amsterdam* crews included just a few from other European countries: Italy, Germany, and Switzerland, to list a few. Lucia's assumption that most of the passengers did not speak English was naïve given the level of education and the empirical data found on passenger lists. Many, if not most, of the passengers were bi-lingual, often listing English as a second language.

There were a number of passengers from Central and South America. Many were merchants, including **Milan Francisco Saravia**, forty-one, a Mexican merchant who recently resided in Cuba, and **Carlos Vidal**, 36, a merchant from Peru.

Her impression that the merchant "will now tour Europe" speaks to her naivety about the looming political situation. The "playboy" may have been trying to impress her, or deflected her questions for other reasons.

She had several photographs of **John Ogden**, thirty-one years old, an American merchant, traveling tourist class, and headed to Leslie Bird on Queen Victoria Street, London.

The *S.S. Nieuw Amsterdam* was a luxurious vessel with the first class restaurant as her most celebrated room, having a Moroccan leather ceiling and Murano-glass lighting fixtures, and columns overlaid in gold leaf. The walls were in Ivory with tinted mirrors, and superb satinwood furniture. This was regarded as one of the finest Art Deco restaurants afloat.

With regard to Lucia's cabin mate, I was unable to find a doctor or a nurse from Austria on the passenger list. However, **Rosa Kuschei** was an Austrian maid, age twenty-seven. People may not have been totally truthful about their occupation, and given that Austria had been annexed by Germany in March 1938, the cabin mate may have felt the need to be cautious in conversation. There also may have been a simple communication problem. There is more about Kuschei in the notes about women on board the May 1939 voyage on page 69.

She saw a 1938 action film, *Heart of the North*, set in Canada with a Royal Canadian Mounted Police (RCMP) hero and produced by Warner Brothers' **Hal B. Wallis**. (More about Wallis later in the story.) Although sound films were introduced in 1900, it was decades before they became commercially available. Seeing one on the ship must have been thrilling.

Lucia's niece, Countess Annabelle de la Panouse (nee Ann Burleigh, born to Lucia's younger sister, Mary Ellen Payton Burleigh), provided a possible explanation for the breakfast item our Aunt Lucia found so distasteful:

> A small commentary regarding the fried bread she was served which may not have been French toast. Fried bread is, for example, commonly served in England as part of the so-called "English Breakfast." Even today a typical country house breakfast offers fried tomatoes, eggs, bacon, herbed pork sausages, bread fried in the bacon fat. Potatoes, toast, juice, tea and coffee, leaving you a choice of going back to bed to digest it all or take off for a couple hours jogging.

> The continental breakfast as served in France is a much lighter affaire of juice, croissants and coffee in comparison to the variations of the so called "EB" served in most northern European countries, where a selection of cheeses and ham may replace the fried bread.

There were several musicians on board and a band master.

Interestingly, the passenger list included **Prince George Cantacuzino**, thirty-nine, an architect, and his wife **Princess Sandra Cantacuzino**, age twenty, who sought passage to London's Royal Court Hotel, and were coming from Roumania {sic}. Each spoke Romanian, French, German, and English. Perhaps she is the "plush horse."

The Prince was chief architect and head of the Roumanian {sic} Commission to the New York World's Fair in 1939, which opened May 30 according to The New York Public Library Digital Collections. He had arrived in the United States on March 8, 1939. He was an avid competitor in aerial acrobatics with his Bücker Bü-133 Jungmeister plane (Romanian champion 1939). This would later help him become Romania's greatest fighter pilot of all time; 608 combat missions and 56 confirmed kills (+ thirteen probable). He flew for the Axis powers initially, but after 1944 shifted to the Allies.

The bride and groom seated at her dining table were **George** and **Mildred Weller,** whom she identified in several photos found in her album.

Frank R. McGibeny, age thirty-six, identified himself as an underwriter from the United States, but he did not specify Lloyd's as his employer.

Also listed was American **Edward David Untermyer,** age thirty-five, a retail stock broker headed to Thomas Cook and Sons on Berkeley Street in London. He was married with two children and lived in Stamford, Connecticut. Thomas Cook & Sons, Ltd was a successful tour/travel agency including cars, railway, and ship voyages. By the time he signed the *World War II Draft Registration Card, 1942* (Old Man's Draft) in February, 1942, he owned his own securities business on Wall Street. Clearly, a successful man. It is noteworthy that he was a Christian.

Later in my research, I chanced to read an article in the June 2018, *Smithsonian* about artwork looted by the Nazis. The article referenced a Samuel Untermyer, who was Edward's uncle. Samuel Untermyer was a corporate lawyer with a reputation for advocating for stock market regulations, government ownership of railroads, and various legal reforms. He was a well-known Zionist leader who was President of Karen Hayesod, the agency through which the movement continues to operate. He also served as attorney for Herman Bernstein's suit against Henry Ford for anti-Semitism. Samuel's father, Isadore Untermyer, was a lieutenant in the Confederate Army in the State of Virginia, having emigrated from Bavaria in the early 1800s.

Lloyds of London is not an insurance company but a society of members, both corporate and individuals, who underwrite in syndicates on the behalf of professional underwriters accepting risk. They create a market of insurance companies which then are able to use the trusted and prestigious Lloyds of London name. Supporting capital is provided by investment institutions, specialist investors, international insurance companies, and individuals.

The identity of the "Chinese girl" remains a mystery. I found no Chinese names on the passenger list. Lucia either was mistaken about the young woman's ethnicity or she had a westernized name. Her use of the term Chinese "girl" would have been acceptable in 1939, and may not have referred to the actual age of the person.

Upon further research, one Cabin Class couple does provide a connection to China. **Joseph C. Gillon-Fergusson** was traveling with his wife, **Elfrida,** a woman sixteen years his junior. He was a banker employed with the famous Hong Kong and Shanghai Banking Corporation (HSBC) founded in 1865, offering services from private banking to global banking. He was on leave from the HSBC at the time. The couple resided in China and were two of three passengers with an apparent association with China.

Further personal communication from the HSBC Senior Archives Manager elicited the following:

Fergusson was an Agent in Hankow during the Second World War. The city was occupied by the Japanese early on (1938), but the Bank was left to run without interference until 8 January 1942. The Bank had pretty much been cut off from the world in terms of banking, so business was more or less limited to local transactions. The management staff (Eastern or Foreign staff recruited from the UK) was decreased to just two men, Fergusson and E. C. Hutchinson. At some point Fergusson and his wife were placed under house arrest and then interned. An agreement to repatriate Japanese in Australia led to some openings for internees to be repatriated through Shanghai and Lourenco Marques. The first group went down river in June 1942 and Fergusson and his family were amongst them. (Taken from King, Frank. *The History of the Hong Kong and Shanghai Banking Corporation, vol. 3, The Hong Kong Bank between the Wars and the Bank Interned 1919-1945: Return from Grandeur,* pg. 582, 583.)

There is a longer discussion of the ship referenced above, the *Tatsuta Maru*, the Japanese transport ship, in a later section about famous people aboard the *S.S. Nieuw Amsterdam*.

Cruise ship socializing

Aunt Lucia seated next to Frank Mc-Gibeny, whom she called "Mr. Mac."

The elaborate wide, six-page fold-out, *Tourist and Third Class Plan* provided to passengers, and found in her scrap book, contained a detailed layout by deck of all cabins and entertainment areas. Aunt Lucia's accommodations included access to the Promenade Deck and access to the Tourist Class sports deck with portable swimming pool, a promenade, verandah, café, a bar with a small orchestra pit, lounges, saloon, and children's playhouse. On the Lower Promenade Deck, she could enter a smoking room, sit in another lounge or walk along the glass enclosed promenade.

Sleeping quarters (Cabin Class, Tourist Class, and Third Class) were located on Decks A, B, and C. Ship stewards and stewardesses were quartered on all three decks. Although her exact cabin is not indicated, A-Deck also included the Tourist Class Dining Saloon to which passengers could take an elevator or just descend a few steps. The Main Deck had another lounge, a writing room/library, a bar, and a smoking room. It also housed the Surgeon's office with waiting room, and the offices for the Chief Seward/Assistant Chief Steward, and the Purser with safe deposit boxes available for passengers' use.

Aunt Lucia appeared to have a history of being the life of the party! A newspaper clipping pasted in her junior high/high school scrapbook was taken from her high school newspaper, *The Gleaner*. The article is entitled: "Class Bequeaths School Treasures. Class of 1933 To Be Success In Many Fields; Industrial and Dramatic...We, the seniors of Wayzata High School, being of sound mind and body (such as it is) do hereby make and ordain this as our last will and testament...Lucia Payton with pleasure leaves her "gift of gab" to Einar Ryden..."

And in another short clipping entitled: *Hall of Fame* {the Girls column}, Lucia Payton is named the *Noisiest*, and *The Biggest Clown*, and *Biggest Chatterbox*. She "won" more titles than any other female classmate that year!

It appears that Aunt Lucia's outgoing personality, humorously recognized in high school, served her well as she enjoyed the people and various activities aboard *S.S. Nieuw Amsterdam*. She was not shy, to be sure.

Two dinner menus, prepared in anticipation of a cruise by *S.S. Nieuw Amsterdam* in mid-September 1939, had themes: the first was A *Prehistoric Repast* and the second was *A Repast in the "Renaissance."* Apparently, eating dinner became an event. Each offered six courses from hors d'oeuvres to desert, with entrees as elaborate as chicken roasted on a spit (with potato chips), veal, Halibut, vegetables, and salads followed by ice cream, cake, and fruit. Each meal was elaborate and passengers were expected to "dress" for meals. Potato chips apparently were still a novel food item in 1939. They originated at a resort in Saratoga Spring, New York, in 1853, and were created by a Native American cook.

Typical activities available to passengers included: deck tennis, swimming, deck golf, dancing, walking along the promenade, shuffleboard, and dining and dancing. Deck chairs were assigned to passengers.

Upon arrival on May 29, 1939, *S.S. Nieuw Amsterdam* carried 227 passengers, of whom 166 were aliens (the majority Americans) and 61 were British subjects.

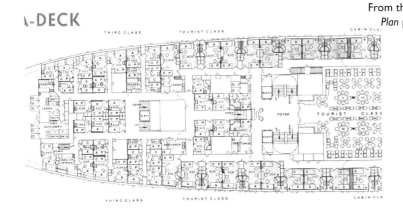

A-DECK

From the brochure *Tourist and Third Class Plan* provided to all of the travelers.

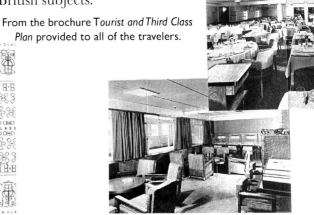

3rd Day (Thursday, May 24)

Was sick one hour last night but not from the ship – I was getting ready for the dance all dressed in my white lace, when all of a sudden my nail polish flew off the dresser all over me & the cleaner on the boat can't get it out. A dutch {sic} lady had a pill made of refined coal she gave me & it did wonders.

I danced most of the night except when we looked at the moon, no smart cracks Duke, the moon looks different on the h2o.

Thursday

What a day – I found the captain & had my picture taken with him, he is a jolly old Dutchman & think of it folks I crashed first class, walked around like I owned the "jernt" and stood at the very front of the boat, what a sight the sun shining on the water & flying fish all around us. They have real wings too.

We are in the gulf stream now so it is very warm in fact everyone is sun burned & the sun never sets until after nine at night.

Beside our huge meals they serve lunch every morning and afternoon, but I eat every time they come around, should do something don't you think.

Aunt Lucia with the children she loved so much - Jon Rieke on the left, and William "Spanky" Rieke, in March 1938.

We have a French diplomat here also who is just returning from Washington, D. C. he has a long black beard & is very P. G.

Am I ever fooling you Duke – haven't missed a meal & eat big ones too. Tonight I had crab meat cocktail & chicken roasted over a spit besides the other three courses.

You folks must plan a trip on this ship, you'll love it & how I wish you were here – you would have fun Duke talking to these people.

I let the people at the table see my pictures of Spanky (William "Bill" Rieke, Jr.) and Jon (Reike's younger brother), but don't dare look at them myself – there are so many little ones here that I can't help wishing I had Spanky.

What a life, am I ever getting spoiled, you never look at your watch because time means nothing. They ring chimes for meals & wait on you so much I expect them to eat me for too.

Oh boy! I won six dollars in my first game at Keno tonight & my friend won eight –

Merle, you would love dancing on deck it's wonderful. I'm so happy & full of steam I can hardly stand it.

I'm writing this morning in our writing room that is also the library – it's very lovely with thick rugs & little desks & chair around the wall.

I stood on deck last night & saw rain falling a mile away, as the storm drew near each wave had a white cap that looked like an Indian in full head dress riding like crazy, it was the most fascinating sight. It is still raining this morning & the old ship is rolling & Duke in spite of it all I ate a very big breakfast.

I am having my hair fixed this morning – Later – a Dutch fellow did it all in curls on top of my head so that the waiters & stewards are making believe they don't know me, asking madam if she isn't at the wrong table.

This Lloyds of London person thinks I have some "light finger" blood in me because I carry off so much stuff to remember the trip by, told me he had a job for me – that he brought his tux but forgot the studs, said it would be easy for me to get some for him but for God's sake leave the bailey until we get to England.

I took some moving pictures this morning of the Americans talking to a bearded Dutchman - it's fun - think I'll get a camera like that myself.

I forgot to tell you about our pool – the waves are so high, because of the rolling of the ship that the water goes over your head most of the time – and is it salty?

Tonight when I was leaving the dining room – a young man at our table said – "hey! Lucia, as long as your {sic} taking silver, you better put it out of sight," & here was a soup spoon in my pocket, the Lloyds fellow did it without my knowing it. The chief steward came over & said, "You can't take silver from the room." For a moment I thought he ment {sic} it – by that time the entire room was roaring.

Someone just called me to see the sun go down, it was beautiful like a huge ball of fire just dropping in the ocean, it is twenty minutes after nine & still light enough to read –

Sunday morning (May 27, 1939)

Won another prize last night & believe it or not, I won the prize dancing. I still can't believe it – must have been a put up job. Everyone is pointing me out as the lucky one.

Drank my first sherry too & played Keno again. I didn't lose any money though because my American friend insisted on paying for my cards, so I think, "OK sap."

Got to bed at four a.m. & slept until twelve but Sunday is the same as any other day on ship, except for our church this morning, I did miss the Tribune (newspaper, Minneapolis, Minnesota) though. This is a very little thing when I think how much I wish you were all here.

We get into Plymouth tomorrow and I have a lot of packing to do again so will write from my Aunt's house.

You can answer this letter & send it to the address on the envelope for I'm anxious to hear from you.

Oceans of love,   Lucia

P.S. Save these pictures for me please – that really is an England Jew standing by me, he wanted his picture taken too, the sailor can't speak English, but knew what to do with his right arm. Pictures are developed on board.

Comments about Letter 2, the third day

The dress she worried so about was the one she wore six years earlier when she graduated from high school in 1933 and again in 1935 as seen in photos at end of the story. Cruising in the 1930s was in an age when passengers did not have to be told how to dress for travel nor at what cruise lines call a "formal" night. Travelers considered that getting there was half the fun in an era when travel was an event and not a nightmare. There was a feeling of gentility among the passengers and activities were geared to promote that feeling.

Lucia is photographed standing with **Captain Abraham Filipo**, a ships Master in the 1920s and 1930s. During WWII he was stuck in Holland and joined resistance work. He set up De Zeemanspot, a sort of bank that ensured that families of Merchant Navy people could survive. He managed to maintain an illegal financial network that was never found out by the Nazi occupiers.

P.G., the term she used to describe a man, is short hand for "pregnant" so I think she is referring to his weight. I did not find a specific French person who was a diplomat nor a person who described his occupation as "diplomat" on the passenger list. However, Aunt Lucia did have a photo of two men, one of whom is portly and bearded, who she identified as "French diplomat and Ogden" in the caption. On the reverse of the photo, she had written "a Dutchman."

Travel by ship prior to the 1960s, was a more serious and demanding experience. Passengers had to have social skills because much of the entertainment was based on the personal interactions of the passengers. There were large lounges where people met and conversed, passenger lists given as souvenirs to see what friends were aboard, formal ballrooms, office tables, the ship's pool, and ceremonies when the ship crossed the Equator.

Aunt Lucia's focus on regularly eating or eating large meals reflects the nutritional deprivation she faced as a child. Also, her childhood scrapbook contains newspaper clippings of food, meals and table settings which I interpret as a child imagining what her future home would have in it. She clearly appreciated eating aboard the ship. She would have taken advantage of the bouillon served mid-morning to tide the passengers over until luncheon was served.

Keno is a lottery-like gambling game. Players wager by choosing numbers between 1 and 80 then twenty numbers are drawn at random. From the excitement in her letter, it is clear Aunt Lucia liked playing the game.

It is not clear who her American friend is, but she included a photo of **Raymond Friend**, age thirty-eight, a U. S. lawyer headed to 163 Queen Victoria Street, E. C. 4, London. He is standing next to **John Ogden** in the photograph. Her use of the term "friend" may have been a play on words. Raymond Friend returned to the United States on June 12, 1939.

On the back of this group photo of a crewmember, Aunt Lucia, the Jewish Englishman and **George Weller**, she wrote: "How do you like my Jew friend? 'Oh man'."

Raymond Friend and John Ogden, May 1939.

Sailor, Aunt Lucia, Larry Lawrence, George Weller, May 1939.

She also wrote this on the back of a second and very small photo: "The American woman and man on here are the just married couple {identified as George and Mildred Weller}. The Jew told us he was an Englishman and I couldn't tell the difference for a few days."

At this point in learning about my aunt, I was surprised to see her statement about "an England Jew." Her observation opened the door in my research about just who were the other passengers and what were their stories. Aunt Lucia's comments about the Jewish man reflect both her apparent fascination with him and mirror broad anti-Semitism prevalent in the United States. Her attitude is likely one she learned from her natal home. Further, anti-Semitism was rife in Minneapolis where she lived at the time. The *Afterwords* continue the discussion about the number of Jewish passengers aboard the *S.S. Nieuw Amsterdam* both going to England and, in particular, returning to New York two and a half months later. At this point, however, it is clear that Aunt Lucia has no real idea of how many Jewish people were her fellow passengers; research on the passenger lists revealed a large number, logical for the time.

This peculiar double image shows Larry Lawrence, Mildred Weller, Aunt Lucia on the left, and George Weller, Aunt Lucia and Larry Lawrence in the right photo.

Arrival in Somerset, England

There is a gap in correspondence from May 25 to May 31, 1939. She arrived in Plymouth, England on May 29, 1939, so presumably, she needed time to settle in at her Uncle's home in Somerset before she wrote again.

On May 31, 1939, Vyacheslav Molotov addressed the Supreme Soviet and denied that the Soviet Union would align itself with Western powers against Nazi Germany. Hitler took this lie as a sign that he should move forward with his plans to conquer Europe.

On May 31, Aunt Lucia wrote Letter 3 on stationery from the Hotel McAlpin New York, but crossed through the name of the hotel. Likely, she took several sheets from the hotel to use for later correspondence.

Letter 3, May 31, 1939 (Wednesday)

Dearest Merle & Duke,

England is just as you read about, old stone walls on each side of very narrow roads & stone houses covered with ivy. The country is very hilly, and all the fields, or downs as they call it, are full of butter cups.

My Uncle Will's (William Alfred Payton) house is stone with roses climbing over it & a huge oak tree is growing right through the stone wall that is built around the house.

My Uncle Dick (Victor Llewellyn Payton) took me through the old Dundry Tower Church (St. Michael the Archangel) where he is now sexton & where grandfathers for four hundred years have been the same, had me

Aunt Flo and Uncle Will Payton at
Oak Tree Farm.

sit in the seat they occupied & showed me their graves, I really had the creeps when I left there.

The church was built in the fourteenth century & I can believe that for deep grooves are worn in the floor & steps, the stones look very black & it smells damp, musty & ages old in there. There are stone steps leading to the top of the Tower which is very high. Uncle is going to take me to the top, but I'll bet there is an army of bats up there beside a few ghosts. Oh man!

The sun has been shining every day & it looks very dry in places.

I climbed to the top of Dundry hill where you can see the mountains of Wales many miles away & all the land between looks like a huge patchwork quilt, because each man has a thorn hedge around his land & the pieces each one owns is a funny patch of green.

Uncle Will has two riding horses so I'm happy as you might know – he also promised to take me to London next week. And Duke I've been asking about your pipe, there is a man in Bristol who makes beautiful handmade ones so I shall look at them someday soon & use my own judgement or if you have any ideas write them to me.

Uncle Dick and Lucia. She is wearing
jodhpurs, riding attire popular
in the 1930s.

It is so peaceful here that it is hard to get used to after the ship but it will do me good.

I miss Spanky & Jon so very much that I don't dare think of them without getting weepy & give my love to Marie & tell her to be good. I won't say how much I wish you were at least near not five thousand miles away.

My uncles are really going to spoil me in fact Will looks in my room each morning to see if I'm still there he says he can't believe it yet.

Please write very soon.

Oceans of love to all of you.   Lucia

Comments about Letter 3

Oak Tree Farm was located in Bishopsworth, Somerset County. From the *1939 Register,* I learned that William A. Payton owned a dairy farm and was a butcher; his work was considered to be *Heavy Labour*, a category assigned by the British government. My Great Uncle Will was born December 28, 1877, and his wife, Florence Elizabeth Cantle Payton, was born April 27, 1889. She was considered to have *Unpaid Domestic Duties*, which meant she was a wife who kept house for the family. Their son, Cecil Harold Payton, was a *Master Butcher*, and lived with his wife in Bristol.

Great Uncle Dick's property was called *Drinagh* according to the notation in Lucia's photo album. The term is Irish and refers to a parish in County Cork, Ireland. Why he named his property this is unknown.

Dundry Tower

Dundry Tower,
St. Michael the Archangel Church.

Of significance to the Payton family in the United States is St. Michael's the Archangel Church in Dundry where generations of Payton ancestors worshipped back to the mid-1500s and many Payton family members are buried in the church cemetery. I verified the families' church activities by searching the original hand-written records from the *Transcription of Church Records*, which includes christenings, marriages, and burials in Dundry from 1558 to 1647. The script, written by church ministers or sextons, was challenging to decipher, but the information firmly established the Payton family as integral to the life of the church.

Further, my third cousin, Jane Day Hamblin wrote, "The position of sexton at St. Michael's has been followed through the generations. Victor Llewellyn was sexton as long as I can remember and until we moved from Dundry I had been a churchwarden for 14 years!!" Jane is the granddaughter of Victor L. Payton. A sexton looks after a church and churchyard, sometimes acting as bell-ringer, and formerly as a gravedigger.

Much of the information about St. Michael's the Archangel Church in Dundry was gleaned from on-line resources. Essentially, the tower was built around 1484 as a landmark visible from many parts of Avon. The four-stage tower is ninety-seven feet high and is a prominent feature in its hill-top position. It is supported by buttresses and is topped by four corner turrets with a polygonal northeast stair turret. The earliest of the six bells in the tower was made in 1642. The church itself consists of a nave, chancel, and chapel with north and south aisles all surmounted by slate roofs. The churchyard contains at least fifty members of the Payton family, and those who married into the clan.

Lucia's father often mentioned to his grandchildren, including me, that he had "rung the bells in the Dundry Tower." I learned that there are about six thousand one-hundred churches with four or more change ringing bells, mostly in England with some in other British colonies. The history of change ringing is particularly English and was developed after Henry VIII left the throne. The early part of the 17th Century saw the start of change ringing using three or four or more bells. Each bell is a different note in the music scale, and they are rung in a mathematical sequence, a learned pattern which is repeated. So, change ringing is the art of ringing a set of tuned bells in a series of mathematical patterns called "changes." Bell ringing is a strenuous activity and ringers are expected to devote hours and years to this service. The Paytons were bell ringers, including Lucia's father before he joined the British Army's Royal Artillery in 1897, and subsequently served in the Boer War. In Lucia's Letter 4 she refers to her experience watching the bell ringers, which she found unsettling.

Reconstruction of the Dundry church has been underway since 2015, but had to be delayed in between spring and fall, 2016, because the roof is used as a roost by the small *Pipstrelle* bats that favor cracks and crevices in new and old buildings for their summer roost and the church membership chose to protect them. They are the smallest bats in England. So, Aunt Lucia was right!

The *1939 Register* indicates that Victor Llewellyn Payton was born on April 27, 1887, was married and was a *Heavy Metal Worker* at Mesare Bapper Pass, Bristol. He lived with his wife Alice Louisa Sidwick Payton, who was born January 1, 1886, and who did *Unpaid Domestic Duties*. There were five people in that 1939 household.

Jane Day Hamblin wrote in her December 27, 2015, and February 15, 2016, emails, "My granddad Victor L Payton worked in a foundry/steelworks so was exempt from serving in the forces. He was part of the Homeguard."

The Home Guard was a defense organization of the British Army during the Second World War. Operational from 1940 until 1944, the Home Guard was composed of 1.5 million local volunteers otherwise ineligible for military service: too young or too old to join the services, or those in reserved occupations. They were to act as a secondary defense force in case of invasion by Nazi Germany and its allies. They were to try to slow down the advance of the enemy, even by a few hours, in order to give the regular troops time to regroup. The Home Guard continued to guard the coastal areas of the United Kingdom and other important places such as airfields, factories, and explosives stores until late 1944 when they were stood down, and finally disbanded in December 1945.

Wales and the Bristol Channel

The Black Mountains are a group of hills in southeastern Wales. Hedge rows were a common natural outline used also in northwestern France to mark fields or property lines. Their presence created exceptional problems for advancing Allied troops after their landing on Normandy Beach in 1944. Discussion of these natural barriers to troop movements may be found in any number of historical accounts of that invasion.

Cardiff, the capital of Wales, located across the Bristol Channel, and due west of Bristol, was a large industrial area and a port town, through which tons of coal passed – it was one of the largest coal ports in the world. It was bombed on January 2, 3 and 10, 1941, by the Nazi *Luftwaffe* bombers (Dornier DO-17, Junkers JU-88, and Heinkel HE-111) in retaliation for the British bombing of Bremen, Germany. The high explosive bombs, incendiary bombs, and parachute mines made this Cardiff Blitz massively destructive, especially the latter two types which were indiscriminant and expedient. Bremen had been Germany's second largest port and housed docks and factories, so it became a prime target for the British bombers.

Lucia may have been referring to clay pipes when she mentioned seeking a gift for Duke Rieke. England had a successful clay pipe industry going back to the 16th Century. Bristol was exporting pipes by 1597 and there were other pipe-making villages in northeast Somerset. Interestingly, there is a pipe-making connection to Lucia's mother Eugenie Ann Hollis Payton. Eugenie's mother, Susan Catherine Smith Hollis, was related to the Gauntletts of Bermuda. The ancestors of the Gauntlett family lived in Wiltshire County, England, and produced clay pipes in Amesbury. Their skill was renowned nationally.

Letter 4, June 6, 1939 (Tuesday)

Dear Merle & Duke,

The weather has been beautiful, the sun is out warm every day. I'm sitting under the rose arbor to write & the whole thing is one mass of flowers.

When the men rang the bells last Sunday, Uncle Dick let me see them do it & did that old Tower shake. I was afraid because one of the bells weighs a ton & there are six of them, I couldn't help thinking how deep it would bury me if one fell on my head.

Sunday afternoon one of my boy cousins took me for a ride over the Mendip hills. When you're on top you can see miles & miles of land fenced in by old stone walls covered with ivy. The walls are built with small stones so it must have taken hundreds of years to get so many miles of it. We rode through Chedder Gourge near the old city of Wells. There is a winding road through the gourge & the rocks tower over you two hundred & fifty feet. They look like tall green palaces because they are all covered in ivy too.

This city of Wells was made by the Romans when they tried to civilize the English "way back when" – so these are a few buildings left of old Roman architect. The thing that impressed me most was an old castle built in a moat, the old draw bridge is still at the door & swans swim around it. Low on one side is a small bell that the swans ring when they want food, & the old monks, that live there now, feed them.

An old man discovered some caves near here, just a few years ago, where they found remains of men who lived two hundred years B. C. The caves are open to the public now so Uncle Will is going to take me through.

We are going to London tomorrow & I'm going well armed with films. Next Sunday my cousin is taking me to Stratford on Avon. It happens that I got my Aunt Celia's {Celia Jane Payton m. Henry Webber} address wrong for she lives at Saltford on Avon, so we will drive to Shakespeare's birth place, spend the day & take pictures.

I took some pictures of the calves & horses for Spanky, they are so tame they follow me around the farm. My uncles & aunts are grand people just full of fun, but we still have a time understanding each other.

Uncle Ted (Edwin "Ted" Coombs m. Lydia Mary "Polly" Payton), who was my Aunt Polly's husband, was already buried when I got here. It was very sudden for I really thought I would see him. Aunt Polly is no better & the folks don't want me to see her.

Uncle Will is having a saddle come today for me, so I'll be riding around to see my other aunts more often.

I'm reading Lorna Doone now because the setting of the story was taken from this part of the country, & it makes it more interesting when you see the places they write about.

I must run along to Bristol to buy some riding clothes so will write more when we come back from London.

Give my love to Spanky & Jon & of course Marie & then I'm sending a special armful to you.

Lucia –

Aunt Lucia reading Lorna Doone, a romantic novel published in 1869 using historical characters and set in Devon and Somerset Counties.

Comments about Letter 4

The Payton men

Lucia's father, Herbert Edwin Payton, rang the church bells when he was a young man as did his father George Payton (1853-1920) of Hawthorne Cottage in Bristol. In 1890 *The Bristol Mercury*, April 8, 1890, Issue 13074 stated: "At the Easter Vestry…it was decided that the office of clerk should be abolished. Mr. G. Payton was elected as sexton and caretaker." In 1895, when George Payton was one of six bell ringers, *The Bristol Mercury*, March 2, 1895, Issue 14604 stated: "Great credit is due to the local ringers for the progress they have made in change-ringing during the winter…"

Further, George's father, William Payton, Jr. (1824-1889) was parish clerk for over thirty-two years. And, William's father, also named William Payton (1797-1875) was listed in *St. Michael's Church Dundry Burials 1813-1887*: "William Payton (Parish Sexton)." Also, in *The Bristol Mercury*, February 10, 1872, Issue 4270, an article thanked local men for playing the church bells and noted that William Payton played treble bells. It is unknown if his father, named William Payton, the Elder, (1770-1860) also served as the church sexton.

Day trips in Somerset

Mendip Hills is a range of limestone hills south of Bristol and Bath in Somerset County running east to west from Weston-super-Mare and Frome. Cheddar Gorge is England's largest gorge with 450 foot cliffs down to stalactite caverns.

Wells is a very small city in North Somerset County and is home to Bishop's Palace and Gardens. A uniquely moated palace, it has an imposing gatehouse with portcullis and drawbridge which give the impression that one may be entering a castle, but inside is a peaceful and tranquil residence.

The cave she visited could be Gough's Cave, located in a deep canyon in Cheddar Gorge in Somerset County. In 1903 the remains of a human male, named "Cheddar Man," were found a short distance inside the cave. He is Britain's oldest complete human skeleton, dating to the Mesolithic, approximately 7150 BCE, which is the Ice Age.

Aunt Lucia standing in front of Windsor Castle.

Aunt Lucia photographed Windsor Castle, St. James Church, the memorial to Lord Nelson at Trafalgar Square, and Big Ben on June 11, 1939.

Lucia was unable to visit her Aunt Lydia Mary Payton Coombs, as her husband, Edwin Coombs had recently passed. Aunt Lydia was Lucia's father's eldest sister, who also died in 1939. Their son is listed in the *1939 Register* as Herbert William George Coombs, born December 22, 1902, and worked as a *Blast Furnace Hand* (Heavy Labour), and was married to Beatrice M. Coombs, born September 28, 1899. She was a *Midwife-Certified M.B.*, and they lived at Bryn Mawr, Crabtree Lane, Dundry.

Celia Florence Mary Coombs Jerred was the daughter of Edwin Coombs. Her husband, Frank R. Jerred, worked as a Painter and Decorator Journeyman, and was born April 5, 1902. He married Celia F. M. Jerred, born January 1, 1905, who worked as *Unpaid Domestic Duties*. Their son, Ronald E. Jerred, b. March 6, 1930, was at school.

On June 6, 1939, when Lucia was enjoying her vacation, King George VI and Queen Elizabeth of England visited the United States, including a state visit to President Franklin D. Roosevelt, becoming the first King and Queen of England to visit the States. The royal trip was encouraged by President Franklin D. Roosevelt to increase popular support for U.S. aid to England as Nazi Germany emerged as a threat in Europe. In addition, on June 23, 1939, the United States Congress established the Coast Guard Reserve, uniformed volunteer units to support the Coast Guard. Clearly, the politicians thought war would be immanent, even if the citizenry on both continents continued to make vacation plans.

Life in Somerset County, England, in the 1930s

Located in southwest England, Somerset is approximately one hundred fifty miles west of London. The county is relatively rural, bounded by rolling hills and featuring large expanses of flat land in the center. The county is famous for its apple orchards and cider production, and in the 1930s was a major producer of willow for the basket making industry.

With so much uninhabited space, Somerset was chosen as the location for a new Royal Ordnance Factory, located between the villages of Puriton and Woolavington. Work began on the factory in 1939 and eventually went on to produce the RDX high explosive required for artillery shell production.

Nearly half a million people lived in Somerset in 1939, most of whom were employed in personal services and agriculture. Today, over 15,000 people work on the farms and orchards in the countryside. Seaside resorts at Minehead and Weston-super-Mare drew vacationers from across the west of England, becoming a major contributor to the local economy and providing seasonal employment.

Despite the county's rural nature, the city of Bath was undergoing major modernization in the 1930s. After a full year without issuing a single license for horse drawn vehicles, the council declared the city fully mechanized. This development coincided with efforts to replace the city's electric tram network with buses, which were thought to be more efficient.

The increasing likelihood of war with Germany was the predominant national concern as the 1930s came to a close, but a conflict further afield brought Somerset onto the world stage earlier in the decade. The invasion of Ethiopia by Italian troops in 1936 forced Emperor Haile Selassie into exile, and he purchased Fairfield House in Bath for his family. The royal family stayed in the area for four years, appealing to the public and global governments to oppose the Italian dictator Benito Mussolini and the Italian invasion of their country.

As elsewhere in England, the movies were a popular pastime with local residents. The then controversial film produced by Warner Brothers, *Angels with Dirty Faces*, starring Humphrey Bogart was banned by the Bath City Council on the grounds that the gangster-themed content could potentially corrupt local youth.

Across the county, people tried to maintain some sense of normality in 1939, even as war seemed inevitable. The County Ground, home of the Somerset Cricket Club, was loaned to the military once the season ended on September 1, 1939. Despite the constant presence of soldiers, the local grounds man ensured that the pitch remained playable in anticipation of the eventual end of hostilities.

Letter 5, June 28, 1939 (Wednesday)

Dear Merle & Duke,

After a long week of rain & fog, the sun finally came out long enough for Uncle Will to make hay. I have been riding the horse rake & learned to drive the horse & tip the rake so well that the men leave me in the field alone while they make hay in another.

The fields are all on the hillside where you can see for miles & such a view I've never seen before. It is very cool though in fact we have feather comforters over us every night & the only time I was really to warm was when Marjory (Marjory Amy Payton, a first cousin) & I had Turkish bath & are they fun!

I saw the play Pygmalion at one of Bristol's oldest play houses it was very good but hard to understand their English.

Last Sunday we went to Stratford on Avon where I saw Ann Hathaway's & Shakespeare's house. Went to the church he attended & it has the most beautiful entrance which is an avenue of trees about a block long making an arch all the way. We had tea on the third floor of Judith Shakespeare's house, they have left it just as it was when she lived there, it has heavy black beams & a very old fashioned fire place. I pinched a tea spoon as a souvenir, I'm getting good at that. I also got a bell, for Lorraine, there and another ash tray for your new house (these I bought).

The church at Bishopsworth (Somerset County) had a carnaval {sic}, one of Dad's (Herbert Edwin Payton) cousins took me. They held a beauty contest & all the contestants looked more or less like "Lizzie." I won the ankle contest with my bow legs so you can guess what the rest must have been like.

Aunty Flo (Florence Elizabeth Cantle m. William Alfred Payton) has a maid that I must tell you about, she weighs over two hundred, wears run over bedroom slippers, she is very short & sloppy & has no teeth, she never walks behind you to pass a dish but always in front & you have to back up or you will get a black eye, everything I do or wear she thinks is funny & gives me a big toothless laugh that makes me shudder.

I have two girl cousins my own age who have boy friends, besides more boy cousins than I can remember, there are more Paytons over here than white people, anyway they all take me out & I believe would get the moon for me if I asked for it, but it seems good to be important for once in my life.

The Germans have begun to raise cain again so all the people around here have been fitted for gas masks, looks like they are going to let the Germans get me for I have none, if it gets any more serious I'll see the American Consulate, although I have already written to London to get my ticket changed to Aug. 4 sailing of the Nieuw Amsterdam but they wrote this morning saying all their ships are full but will try to get me back as soon

Aunt Lucia riding on the hay rack, Oak Tree Farm, Somerset, England.

as possible so you see everyone must be a little nervous if they are filling all ships to America. Uncle was cheerful last night, he said, "I don't see you going back for four or five years with all this trouble coming on." I told him swimming wasn't too bad when there is a war behind me.

All the parks have been torn up for air raid shelters so the place looks pretty wild.

I have been to the Art Institute which is very interesting & this afternoon Uncle is taking me to the zoo (but I'll be careful).

I have been riding but found, much to my surprise, that English women don't ride very much & it is only around London that you see them ride at all. You & I shall get in some riding when I get back and a bit of sailing too I hope.

My friends on the boat have been sending me cards from Germany & Holland, they are all sailing for home before me though.

The gang sent me a letter full of nonsense that made be a bit homesick for them, the rats.

Give my love to Spanky & Jon & Marie and a huge order for you & Duke.

Lucia

Comments about Letter 5

Lucia visited the Bristol Old Vic Theatre, established in 1766, and is the oldest working theater in England.

William Shakespeare was baptized and buried at Holy Trinity Church. He and his wife, Anne Hathaway, had at least three children, the youngest of whom was Judith Shakespeare, who had a twin brother.

The *1939 Register* lists Maud F. Wilson, who was born November 14, 1887, and was employed as a *Domestic Servant*, in the William Payton household. The photograph of her depicts a portly woman, laughing into the camera.

The girl cousins are Marjory Amy Payton, twenty-three, and her sister Isabel Betty Payton, twenty-one, both daughters of Victor Llewellyn "Uncle Dick" Payton.

The Office of the American Consulate in Bristol was housed on Baldwin Street on a peninsula surrounded by a canal. Uncle Will's war prediction was right on target: Britain entered World War II on September 3, 1939, and the war in Europe ended September 2, 1945. Although Aunt Lucia continued to tour England that summer, the tone of her letters changed as she looked forward to returning to the States.

The Museum and Art Gallery she toured was built in 1823, and is now the Bristol City Museum and Art Gallery located on Queens Road. The Bristol Zoo, formerly the Zoological Gardens, opened in 1836, was on Downside Road, all within easy access from Uncle Will's farm.

Lucia was an accomplished rider and mentions only riding with her male cousins. Perhaps women in farming areas, where the Payton families lived, viewed horses as work animals and not for sport riding/sport hunting popular among upper class English women.

These friends may be the bride and groom, George and Mildred Weller, whom Lucia met on board in the dining room in May and of whom she had at least four photos. This Chicago couple sailed the *S.S. Nieuw Amsterdam* again on its July 21, 1939, voyage to the United States, boarding in Boulogne sur Mer, France. Although the Wellers' reasons for a July return cannot be discerned, that Lucia put these comments in the letter about increased German war activity suggests that the Wellers may have wanted to leave Europe before events became more critical. He was an assistant buyer for a mail order house; she was an elementary school teacher as indicated in 1940.

July 6, 1939: German Nazis closed the last Jewish enterprises.

Friends Mildred and George Weller with Larry Lawrence on the deck of the *S.S. Nieuw Amsterdam*, May 1939. They wrote to Aunt Lucia of their departure from Europe in July.

Aunt Lucia loved children so her wanting to be photo-graphed with this adorable boy was not out of character. She is pictured here with Herbert Henke on the ship's deck.

Letter 6, July 21, 1939 (Friday)

Dear Merle & Duke,

Can you spare a little of Minnesota's heat? We can use it & how.

Merle you look lovely & I'm showing your picture to everyone & my folks think you're beautiful, but what makes your dress look so dark? I thought it was iris blue.

All the cities are having air raid practice. When it came to be Bristol's turn I was really scared, just imagine a big city going entirely black, sirens making a terrible noise while planes roared overhead. I really thought the Germans had come.

I have been spending some time at the sea shore in the extreme end of South England. The waves came in six feet high & when the tide is out there are rocks as big as houses all covered with shell fish, sponges, & jelly fish that you can explore for hours. I found a big star fish & was I excited! Thought it was an octopus, in my excitement I stepped back on a jelly fish. They are so slippery my feet flew out from under me & I did a beautiful back dive.

We visited the city of Bath where the Roman baths were found, the water comes out of the rocks boiling hot, just think over 2000 years ago the old boys knew how to make lead pipes to bring this water to the pools they had made for bathing. I learned the history of it all & can tell it better than I can write it.

We also have been exploring caves that are hundreds of feet underground where cave men once lived. Man!, but it's spooky in there. In one place there is hundreds of tons of rock over you & not a thing you can see holding it up. At your feet is a river twelve feet deep running under the rocks & no one knows where it comes from. It's very damp in there & water falls on your head from the river that is flowing on top of the pile of rocks, fine place for a murder I thought & left before anyone else got the idea.

I must tell you about my bed room, a bed so high with feathers that I have to run & jump on it, but very comfortable, there is a fireplace in there also, a wash stand with a pitcher & basin & two lovely pots that all match & one painted with blue roses. I don't know why there are two pots, but have an idea you buy the set like a two pants suit. I want to pinch one to bring home just to show you but thought the Customs might think it strange.

My cousin Harold (Cecil Harold Payton), Uncle Will's only child, is such a nut he never worries about a thing & when we go to those sea side places we see how many ash trays we can pinch. I have him trained now so it doesn't bother him to take them. He has a car so he & his wife (Doris Vera "Peggy" Winstone) take me all over England & have the best times.

I have taken a lot of pictures but they need explaining so that's why I don't send them.

Jon surely looks natural & so does my Spanky. I'll be so glad to see them, I didn't realize how much till the pictures came, by the way I dreamed of you Merle, the other night thought you were standing by my bed with your arms around me & I woke up as darn homesick & lonesome for you that it was pathetic.

Three weeks from this Sunday (July 23), I will be home, my ship sails August fourth. I'll get into Mpls Sunday Aug 13 on the Hiawatha. Will send you a telegram of the time I will get in, you will meet me won't you?

Aunt Flo & Uncle Will are having a party for me the Wednesday before I leave (Wednesday, August 2, 1939) & all the family besides friends will be here, a lady is coming to start the baking a day before so you can imagine all the people they are planning for.

Merle we are going to do an awful lot of swimming to make up for my cold summer when I get home, & horseback riding too –

Now when to the time for me to leave is so near I can hardly wait, yet it will be no easy thing to say good-bye to Uncle Will, he already is going about looking gloomy & wants to hire a bus to take all the family to Southhampton {sic} to see me go.

You won't be able to answer this letter for I will sail four days after you get it, so I'll just start for home & send a telegram.

Oceans of love from your own – Lucia

Comments about Letter 6

Historical weather report excerpts indicated: "There were some warm days at the beginning of July, and on the 4th the temperature rose above 26°C (78.8 degrees Fahrenheit). The month was changeable; rain fell frequently but was mostly light. However, on the 20th, nearly 14mm of rain was measured. After the warm start, temperatures fell to normal or a little below, but after mid-month there were several cool or very cool days. On the 24th, the temperature only rose to 16.2°C (61.16 degrees Fahrenheit), but on the 25th it was sunny nearly all day."

Bristol Blitz

Air raids were not new to Britain as the Germans had bombed the island nation during World War I. The start of the air raid drills in Britain before World War II began after the spring 1938 Munich Crisis, and were orchestrated by the Air Raid Precautions, a British civil defense organization.

Radar had been developed in 1935 and by 1939 radar installations circled much of Britain. When the sirens sounded, citizens had four minutes to take shelter; Nazi *Luftwaffe* aircraft could reach Britain in six minutes.

First bombed in November 1940, Bristol, a city of over 400,000 in the 1930s, was a key target for *Luftwaffe* bombings because it included railways, navigable rivers (Avon and Frome), seaport docks at Bristol Harbor (the largest port city in England on Bristol Channel), Bristol Airport that serviced the island nation, and the Bristol Aeroplane Company. In addition, Bristol was home to metal industries, shipbuilding, engineering, chemical works, smelting, as well as the manufacture of household goods. The *Bristol Street Plan*, a thick brochure published by British Isles Publicity Ltd, Bristol and London, found in Aunt Lucia's album was the source for this information. Because of its strategic importance, Bristol was the 5th most heavily bombed city in England during WWII; the Bristol Blitz consisted of six major bombing raids in 1940-1941.

Home air raid shelters were essential during the Bristol Blitz. The Anderson shelter was designed in 1938 to accommodate six people. They were quite cramped and someone taller than six feet would not have been able to stand up in one. They were made of curved steel panels, and once constructed, the shelters were buried over one meter in the ground and covered over with a thick layer of soil and turf. Approximately 3.5 million Anderson shelters were built either before the war had started or during the conflict. Families were provided with the materials and were expected to construct the shelters from a set of instructions.

My third cousin Jane Day Hamblin's email on August 25, 2016, from Somerset, England provided this information:

You asked about Anderson shelters, I am not aware that many were built in the village but Victor Llewellyn and family including my mum (Isabel) used an underground shelter which Tom Gadd (husband of Hilda Sidwick) built in his paddock. This was situated between the gardens of Uncle Tom and Gran & Grampy (Victor and Alice). It had several steps down into it and was completely tiled. There were what looked like shelves against the wall which were for sleeping either as bunks or sitting on! I have heard mum say that when the sirens sounded they would all run to the shelter and there could be as many as eleven people including children!! A tight squeeze! I think they must have had fun as well - Gran Payton (Alice) had a piano in her hallway at Drinagh, one of the evacuees played the piano and some evenings they would gather in the hallway singing together and not even hear the sirens!

Further, during the Second World War, Bristol's most important aircraft was the Beaufighter, a heavy two-seat multirole aircraft, a long-range fighter, a night fighter, ground attack aircraft, and torpedo bomber. It was used extensively by the Royal Air Force (RAF) and Commonwealth air forces and by the USAAF. The Beaufighter was derived from the Beaufort torpedo bomber, itself a derivative of the Blenheim, a light bomber made by the Bristol Aeroplane Company. Used in the Pacific Theatre as well, the Japanese called the Beaufighter "Whispering Death."

In 1940, shadow factories were set up at Weston-super-Mare for the production of Beaufighters, and underground at Hawthorn, near Corsham, Wiltshire {the county adjacent to Somerset}, for engine manufacture. Construction in the former stone quarry at Hawthorn took longer than expected and little production was achieved before the site closed in 1945. The company's war-time headquarters were in the Royal West of England Academy, Clifton, in Bristol.

Many Bristol families sent their children to safety in the English countryside to live with strangers, as did many families living in London. However, there is no indication the Payton extended family had to do this, as they lived out in the country. In fact the Victor L. "Uncle Dick" Payton family housed evacuees from Bristol and London. Others in the local community housed a group of children from London as well.

Aunt Lucia's photo album chronicles the trip to Bude Bay, located in the extreme south and west of England on Bristol Channel which empties into the Atlantic Ocean. There were other trips with family to Ilfracombe, a seaside resort on the North Devon Coast, Bristol Channel.

Bath is located about eleven miles southeast of Bristol and the Bristol Airport is nearby. The Roman Baths were built around the only hot water springs in England. Celtic Druids thought the site was sacred to the goddess *Sulis*.

Lucia with her first cousin Isabel Betty Payton on a trip to the beach along English Channel.

This photo from Lucia's album shows L-R, Uncle Will Payton, Violet Ablett, Aunt Celia Jane Payton Webber (Will's sister), Aunt Lucia, and Bert Payton, a cousin, just before she left the village for Southampton, on August 4, 1939.

In August 1939, German U-boats and two "pocket battleships" (*Panzerschiff* built by the *Reichsmarine*, were cruisers with large caliber guns), sailed for their war stations in the Atlantic.

After a little over eight weeks in England, Aunt Lucia embarked at the Port of Southampton on her return voyage aboard the *S.S. Nieuw Amsterdam* on August 4, 1939. Ticket #37839. Her stated occupation was "Actress." She arrived at the port of New York on August 11, 1939.

It is interesting that she reinvented herself by giving "actress" as her occupation. No reason was given in her letters. Parenthetically, there were a large number of "Actresses" on board (actually, 8 in total for both voyages). The master of the vessel was **Johannes Jacobus Bijl,** age fifty-eight, of Dutch origin; he had captained the ship on its maiden voyage on May 10, 1938.

She identified her cabin mate under a photo of the two of them having a wagon race on deck on the return trip as **Elsa Otto.** The ship's passenger list states: *Flora D. E. T. Otto, 20, female, single, no occupation, read & write English, German, born in Dresden, Germany, visa #NQIV. 69, issued in Rotterdam. Apr. 20, 1939.* I found no other information about this cabin mate.

Aunt Lucia racing on the deck of the *SS Nieuw Amsterdam* with her cabin mate lagging behind. August, 1939.

Elsa Otto, a German girl and I on deck of Nieuw Amsterdam on my return voyage August 1939.

The following photo is of Lucia and "Jack" Moore. He is **John Paull Moore**, twenty-seven, an American born in Ohio on September 16, 1911, but living in El Paso, Texas. He was a draftsman in a refinery in 1940. She visited him in 1940, among other friends, on her trip to Los Angeles and Long Beach, California. He served as a Lieutenant Commander in the United States Navy during World War II, enlisting on July 3, 1941, and returned to Texas after being released on February 10, 1946. He died on December 24, 2001, and is buried in Fort Bliss National Cemetery. If her body language in the photo of them together aboard the ship is any indication, it seems Aunt Lucia really liked John P. Moore.

John Paull "Jack" Moore and
Aunt Lucia on board ship, May 1939.

On that second-to-the-last Atlantic trip as a luxury cruise passenger liner, *S.S. Nieuw Amsterdam* sailed from Rotterdam (Holland) to Boulogne sur Mer (France), to Southampton (England), and finally to the Port of New York. Upon arrival the *Statement of Master of Vessel Regarding Changes in Crew Prior to Departure* stated: 654 crew, 11 discharged, 102 deserted, and one signed on at port leaving a total of 644 set to sail again. The majority of the crew were Dutch, however there were also crew from Germany, Belgium, Switzerland, United States, and Italy. The crew members varied in their years of service: ¾ year to 50 years, and ranged in age from 15 to 62 years of age.

The voyage also transported aliens to the United States: the *List of Manifest of Alien Passengers for the US* included many "Hebrew" people born in or listed their last place of residence as Germany, France, Holland, Romania, or Poland. Clearly, these passengers barely escaped the horrors of World War II. Another record, *Records of Aliens Held for Special Inquiry* listed two *Polish Hebrews* and three *German Hebrews* whose paperwork (*i.e.*, visa, passport, or health records) was in question and who were cited for "no immunizations" or "general physical was poor." Some traveled in tourist class, and some were berthed in third class accommodations. There were a large number of Jewish refugees on board, including many listed on the separately compiled *Quota Visa* lists.

An Affidavit of Surgeon, completed by Thomas N. Cassidy, MD, with six years' experience, and a graduate of University of Georgetown, Washington, DC, stated he had "personally examined each of eight aliens and attested to their physical and mental health." He signed the form on August 11, 1939.

The United States immigration quota system prevented scores of Jewish refugees from entering the country. "The United States allowed 105,000 refugees from Nazism to enter the country between 1933 and 1940, but this was only a small percentage of those who tried to immigrate (between 1940 and 1944, the record was even worse)." This attitude was discussed in *No Ordinary Time: Franklin and Eleanor Roosevelt – The Home Front in World War II* by Doris Kearns Goodwin, 1994, and cited in Bryan Mark Riggs' *The Rabbi Saved by Hitler's Soldiers*, 2016.

There was increasing pressure for Jewish Europeans to leave their home countries because on January 30, 1939, Hitler called for the extermination of the Jews. Aboard *S.S. Nieuw Amsterdam*, on a separate list of aliens entering the United States, those in the column stamped *Quota Visas* were: seventy-four "Hebrews" boarded ship in Rotterdam, 16 boarded in France and 4 boarded in Southampton. Jewish passengers who were American citizens were not separately identified by their religion as they were not considered to be "alien" when entering the United States. Obtaining a *Quota Visa* was complex, including obtaining documents and personal sponsors, a physical, proof of paid taxes and sufficient monetary support, which had to have taken a great deal of time to collect. The United States Holocaust Memorial Museum listed these requirements, and I calculated each German Jewish adult requesting a *Quota Visa* needed between fourteen and seventeen separate documents to seek an entry visa to the United States in the 1930s and 1940s.

With war on the brink, amazingly the ship set sail again August 15, 1939, for Rotterdam via Plymouth and Boulogne sur Mer. The *S.S. Nieuw Amsterdam*, carrying 1,288 passengers, returned to New York on September 1, 1939, the day Nazi *Wehrmacht* invaded Poland. The ship and its crew were seemingly stranded in the United States.

After only eighteen voyages, she berthed at Hoboken, New Jersey, for a time. During the next several months, she completed two series of cruises in the American hemisphere. Between October 12, 1939, and November 18, 1939, she cruised to Bermuda followed by a cruise on December 23, 1939, to the Caribbean. She kept cruising during the winter 1939/1940.

In May 1940, Holland fell to the Nazis, and by September 1940, the ship was turned over to the British Ministry of War Transport. The original Dutch crew served six years, not returning to their homes until 1946.

S. S. Nieuw Amsterdam, with a nominal troop capacity of 6,800/speed of over 20 knots, was among the British-controlled "monsters" – high-capacity, high-speed troop ships capable of sailing unescorted and thus critical to the build-up in Britain for the invasion of the Continent. She transported over 350,000 troops and steamed around 530,452 nautical miles, and came through World War II unscathed, before being returned to the Holland America Line in 1946. She was demolished in 1974.

August 25, 1939, the United Kingdom and Poland signed an agreement of mutual assistance, meaning that the UK and France, with its separate agreement with Poland, would aid Poland in case of aggression by a foreign power.

September 1, 1939, Hitler invaded Poland, starting the Nazi *Blitzkreig* across Europe. France and England did not come to Poland's aid.

September 3, 1939, England declared war on Germany.

Aunt Lucia riding at Frank T. and Lucia Peavey Heffelfinger's Estate in 1933.

Aunt Lucia was physically very active in the 1930s, especially liking outdoor activities as depicted in her personal 1930s annotated photo album. In 1933, she is photographed astride a pinto and looks comfortable in the saddle wearing her jodhpurs as she rode "at Heffelfinger's home." This vast estate employed members of the Payton family at various times, so it was not unusual for Lucia to be on the property.

The Peavey and Heffelfinger families were involved with the merchandizing and production of grain for flour and feed and were very wealthy. The Peavey-Heffelfinger mansion, *Highcroft*, was located across the street from Lake Minnetonka in Wayzata, Minnesota, on Highcroft Road and Ferndale Road. The mansion was designed by William Channing Whitney, a prominent Minneapolis architect. The estate occupied 111 acres with a 30-room mansion with several out-buildings for horses and cows. Frank Totten Hefflefinger had been a grain merchant since at least 1900 when he was thirty-one and married to Lucia Louise Peavey Heffelfinger. There was one female child in the Heffelfinger extended family whose name was also Lucia. This is noteworthy because Payton family lore says that Aunt Lucia changed her name from Lucy to Lucia to "match the fancy names of rich people in Wayzata." This may very well have been the case and would fit with Aunt Lucia's intentional steps in reinventing herself.

From 1901 to 1946 the freighter *Frank T. Heffelfinger*, built by the Peavey Steamship Company, Duluth, sailed on the Great Lakes, with Duluth as its home port. The Peavey Grain Elevator was constructed in 1900 near Garfield Avenue on Rice's Point, called Grass Island. It was demolished in 1997-1998.

Parenthetically, in 1953, the estate was parceled out and sold to other Ferndale residents according to Wayzata Heritage Preservation Board. This year seemed to be a pivotal year for Aunt Lucia: at age forty-two she joined the Episcopalian Church to marry a widower, William Tunstall Townes, who was a Minneapolis architect, in the same year that a beloved site for her youthful outdoor activities was dismantled.

In 1934, Lucia and her girlfriends swam and camped at Bay Point, Minnesota. There are many Bay Points in Minnesota: Eden Prairie and Red Wing are two examples.

Aunt Lucia traveled across the United States in this decade. Album photos show her in May 1936 on a trip to Ocean Park, California, again traveling with girlfriends. During that initial trip to California, she visited Forest Lawn in Glendale and traveled later to Salt Lake City, Utah.

In 1935, she and girlfriends were photographed during March and April outings "in the woods."

Aunt Lucia posing while camping with friends in 1934 at Bay Point.

In August 1936 she and girlfriends camped "…in a cabin on Lake Superior in Duluth." She returned to camp along the "North Shore of Lake Superior" in the summer 1937. It looks like that trip also took her to Kakabeka Falls in Ontario, Canada. Summer picnics at Como Park, St. Paul, Minnesota, were common.

In February 1938, she and a friend skied on Orchard Hill, Orono, Minnesota. This was followed by a photo of "First Picnic March 13, 1938" and another picnic with a mixed group on Crow River in April that year. In June, she is back riding horses with friends, and, later that summer, sailing with "Duke" Rieke and his family on Lake Minnetonka. In May 1939, prior to her trip to England, she partied with friends, and in October, after her return from England, she and friends picnicked "in the woods."

Aunt Lucia enjoying the beach at Ocean Park, California, May 1936.

Her photo album, so integral to my research, chronicles trips she made in 1940 through 1942 to California, Colorado, and Texas, and includes photos of some of her siblings and their children, as well as her parents.

After World War II, she visited England and her Payton relatives several times. Additionally, she flew Pan American Airways with her husband to Bermuda in July 1958 to visit her mother's ancestral homeland. A trip to France to visit her niece, Annabelle Burleigh (now Countess Annabelle de la Panouse, wife of Count Paul de la Panouse) at Chateau de Thoiry was interspersed with trips to Olympia, Washington, to visit her youngest brother, William Arthur Payton, and his family.

Lucia loved picnics – winter or summer – in the Minnesota woods. She is posing by a pump in March 1935 and on a tree in April 1935.

Lucia along the shore of Lake Superior while camping in Duluth, Minnesota, 1937.

Aunt Lucia getting ready to sail with her close friends Dr. W. William "Duke" Rieke and his wife, Merle, on Lake Minnetonka, summer 1938.

A 1937 photo shows Lucia and "Spanky," a nickname for William "Bill" Rieke, Jr., at the beach in Wayzata. The album caption says, "First swim of the year." Lake Minnetonka, Wayzata, Minnesota, 1937.

In May 1939, just prior to her trip to England, Aunt Lucia joined her friends for a picnic. Nice catch!

Class of 1932-1933, Wayzata High School. Lucia Payton is in second row,
fourth from the left. A fellow student rests her hands on Lucia's shoulders.
The teacher, standing at the far left, is Mr. M. G. Gullickson.

Lucia Payton in her graduation dress, taken either
spring, 1933 or later in 1935 "in the orchard."
She inserted the above image into the cover of
her 1930s photo album, one separate from the
album she kept documenting her trip
to England in 1939.

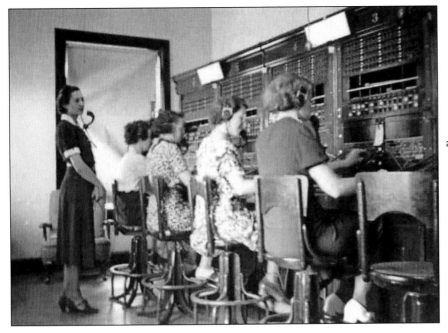

Telephone Exchange, Northwestern Bell, Minneapolis, Minnesota. Lucia Payton is seated second from the right. About 1938-1940. This one-square-inch photo, found in Aunt Lucia's album, was enlarged for the story. This seems to depict a training station for new operators.

End Note

Lucia Sydney Payton married William "Bill" Tunstall Townes in St. Martin's by the Lake Church (Episcopal) on Lake Minnetonka, Minnesota, on June 27, 1953, just twenty-eight days after she was confirmed in that church. He was a successful architect and a widower having lost his first wife in November 1950. Bill and Lucia were god-parents to Isabel Payton Hamblin's grandson, Michael John Hamblin. The Somerset branch of the Payton family kept in touch with Aunt Lucia for many years. Lucia and her husband traveled to Bermuda and France and she made several more trips to England in her later years. Bill and Lucia lived in Wayzata until his death in 1989. Aunt Lucia maintained her ties with friends in Wayzata and belonged to the Wayzata Historical Society. She moved to St. Paul after Bill's death. When she died on March 18, 2009, she was eight months short of her ninety-eighth birthday. Her remains are with Bill at Lakewood Cemetery, Minneapolis, Minnesota.

NOTES ON ANTISEMITISM IN MINNESOTA IN THE 1930S

Given Aunt Lucia's particular remarks about one fellow passenger who was Jewish, I think it necessary to briefly describe life in Wayzata, Minnesota, in the 1930s. I also grew up in that small town, just fifteen miles west of the Twin Cities in the 1950s and 1960s. I recall a split in community life based on religion and socio-economic status, and ethnicity. Certainly there were no Jewish people or African Americans residing in Wayzata until the Civil Rights movement of the late 1960s. Quite simply, Wayzata was segregated in many ways.

For my aunt to interact with a Jewish man in the heady context of cruise life must have been exciting for her, and confusing given the antisemitism to which she was undoubtedly exposed as a child and young professional woman. Even at that, her own latent prejudice did come through in her comments about **Larry Lawrence**. She was unaware, apparently, that scores of her fellow passengers were labeled "Hebrew" on the passenger lists.

I was intrigued by my aunt's having specifically identified a male passenger by his faith, then commenting in a biased fashion about him in Letter 2, the portion dated Sunday, May 27, 1939. She lived in Minneapolis in the 1930s and 1940s, a time when antisemitism was rife. In a recent Minnesota Public Radio rebroadcast on December 2017 of a 1992 interview with elderly Jewish leaders in the Twin Cities, including my former mother-in-law, Fanny Schwartz Schanfield, it was stated that Minneapolis was the "capital of antisemitism in the 1930s," and mirrored national sentiment. There were covenants and restrictions placed on Jewish residents with regard to owning property, obtaining jobs, and accessing health care. Dayton's, 3M, and Pillsbury were cited as companies that did not hire Jews. The basis for Jewish economy at the time was as merchants since they could not get corporate jobs. Discrimination was legal. There is no way my aunt was unaware of this situation.

NOTES ON CRUISE LINE PASSENGER LISTS

I researched the lives of virtually every passenger on both voyages in my quest to add bits of culture and history to this story. Some names were very common (into the thousands) and without other corroborating data, could not be included here. Also passenger lists did not contain corroborating information for married women traveling without their husbands or children, making their brief stories untold. Other women, labeled "Housewife" were included after I researched more thoroughly to find their husband's name. Yet, basic genealogical searches were difficult in some cases, and the scarce bits of data did not add measurably to the telling. I took the easy road and simply eliminated those names that proved too problematic to pursue. In doing so, I surely may have missed telling about one famous or influential person or another; my apologies to their descendants.

Passenger names and personal data were recorded in a seemingly endless variety of ways, which I especially noted on the return trip to New York. Basically, passengers were identified primarily as Cabin, Tourist, or Third Class; secondarily, many were listed again as Quota Immigrants Cabin Class Passengers or Quota Visas Third Class. These latter were mainly "Hebrews" as indicated under the column entitled "Race or People." In all classes, the U.S. born American citizens were asked for their home address, while naturalized citizens added the date for their naturalization. They were not asked to answer "Race or People." Cabin Class passengers who were not American citizens (*List or Manifest of Alien Passengers* for the United States Immigrant Inspector at Port of Arrival) were asked to answer "Race or People." Responses in these cases ranged from "English," "German," "Scotch," and "Lithuanian" to "Hebrew." Again, the differentiation between nationality, ethnicity, or religion is exemplified on these records.

For example, two Tourist Class passengers appeared on the *Record of Aliens Held for Special Inquiry*. **Chaskiel Kalb** was a "Polish Hebrew" merchant who lived in Paris, spoke French, whose passport was extended thirty days. He was admitted to the United States three days after the ship arrived at the Port of New York on August 11, 1939. After the war ended, he identified himself as a citizen of Argentina, and traveled extensively from that country to Europe.

Ernst Schwarz, his wife and child, reportedly had "health issues," but all were admitted to the United States on August 12, 1939. I can only imagine the angst felt by those who had traveled so far, only to be held up for a few more days before being admitted to the country.

As I worked with the passenger information, I realized the unique perspective I had in doing historical and genealogical research: I knew what happened to each passenger before she or he had actually lived the events. With this perspective, I understood why some people changed their names or listed their occupations inaccurately. When boarding a ship, passengers entered a different world where few people knew each other. When leaving the dock, this floating new world became all the more real as it was made up of new experiences and the possibility of making new friends, and the experience allowed each person to become someone else – even for just seven days. The life on board was artificial. It was an island with its own little community creating a perfect atmosphere for each person to be who she or he wanted to be.

As the story of the travelers unfolded, it became apparent that many of Aunt Lucia's fellow passengers were not just successful, wealthy, or well educated, they were exceptionally so. Several of these people went on to lead privileged lives likely because their social rank and advanced education allowed them to do so. There were scientists, bankers, medical personnel, college professors, merchants, and religious leaders, whose personal and professional success was nothing short of stellar.

And, there they all were – on a voyage with a telephone operator from Wayzata!

AFTERWORD PART I

Men aboard the *S.S. Nieuw Amsterdam* on its voyage to England in May 1939.

As I worked with her letters, scrapbooks, and photos I learned that Aunt Lucia had a photo for virtually every statement or person she mentioned in her letters. She apparently wanted photos of people she spoke to, dined with or with whom she attended events on board or on day trips in England. With that in mind, the trip to England and its importance to her became more apparent. The people she met were very well educated, both academic and professional, including the women, had upper-class occupations, and many were seasoned world travelers. She must have realized how far out of her league she was. The following vignettes of some of her fellow passengers set the socio-cultural backdrop for her voyage to England.

The voyages to and from England each took about eight days. It would have been easy for passengers to learn about each other as many cruise lines handed out passenger lists as a souvenir before boarding. Other cruise lines placed a list in each cabin for each passenger. All of this was done to assist passengers in making acquaintances. In addition, nearly all the larger vessels – and the *S.S. Nieuw Amsterdam* was one of those – printed a small newspaper with "local" gossip, articles contributed by passengers, and sometimes there was a good bit of talent on board. The paper would also have announced plays, concerts, games, and movies. Social interaction occurred over meals, touring the decks, participating in games, and simply talking to one another. Social skills were a must.

Since my aunt was an outgoing and gregarious young woman on an adventure – 'daring' to go up to the First Class deck aboard the ship – it seems reasonable that she spoke with many of her fellow passengers, not just those assigned to Tourist Class. Did she have the social awareness to focus her conversations on only the Cabin and Tourist Class passengers, eschewing interaction with those traveling Third Class? Who knows? She dressed stylishly herself and surely would have noticed the clothing of other passengers, and probably drew conclusions about social status based on apparel, as she did when writing about the overweight woman on the train from Minneapolis to Philadelphia (see Letter 1). She would have noted the women's jewelry and could have drawn conclusions about class standing on that basis. She would have been able to differentiate between the "ladies" and their "maids." Further, meals were served in class-segregated dining rooms. With all this in mind, I continued to research other passengers whom she at least encountered frequently, and with whom she may have spoken. She was not afraid to approach anyone for conversation. The passengers and their activities became part of the culture on board and their stories provide a historical context for her story. From the excited tone of her letters, her statement that she was so happy on board the ship, and that she relished being waited on relate clearly that this young woman was open to adventure and soaking it all in.

She mentioned in Letter 3 that she met a diplomat. The closest link I could find was **Walton Platt Ryder Mawdsley,** born April 12, 1904, from Formby Lanes, Redcroft, who identified his occupation as "Consul." He was a solicitor (lawyer) as well. He was born into a wealthy family, headed by his widowed mother, who lived by "private means" in 1911. He grew up in a household with servants such as maid, nurse, cook, and waitress according to the *Census of England and Wales, 1911, #162.* Mawdsley traveled extensively in the 1930s and again in 1952, at a minimum, to such countries as the United States, Gibraltar, Canada, Bahrein, and Yemen, presumably performing his duties as consul, although the exact nature of his travel cannot be ascertained.

As mentioned before, Lucia was photographed aboard ship standing next to someone she identifies as "…a real England Jew." It looks like they are posing on the first class deck with **George and Mildred Weller** as indicated on the back of the photo, where she had written "Mr. & Mrs. Geo. Weller," and below that the name "Larry Lorance" (or, perhaps, Lawrence). From the photo, I estimated the age of the Jewish man to be in his late twenties to late thirties. The intriguing "English Jew" may have been **Albert Lawrence** (with the nickname "Larry"), the closest name I could find to match what Aunt Lucia had penciled on the back of his photo. Finding the correct man, in this case, was a problem as there were so many men in England with the name "Albert Lawrence," that the research bogged down. However, I do know that he traveled to England earlier in May 1939, and presumably returned to the United States, only to sail again to England May 21 and arriving on May 29, 1939. On those trips, and an additional one in 1949, he stated again that he was a "Director" but of what is not known. He remains a history mystery.

A review of the passenger list for British citizens disembarking in England the end of May 1939, brought at least six names of other Jewish men from that age group. I researched each name to find additional data about their travels in the 1930s to countries outside of England. In that time all passengers who were not citizens of the country to which they sailed were considered "aliens." I looked for a designation of "Hebrew" or "Jewish" and initially found four British men identified by their "Race or People" as "Hebrew." Later, I realized there were dozens more Jewish people listed as "Hebrews." As noted below, all passengers on the Alien lists (non-citizens entering any port) were asked their "Race or People." It seems reasonable that some Jewish passengers would defer that definition to "English" or "French" or "American" in lieu of identifying themselves as possible refugees. This makes sense in light of the strict quota the United States imposed on Jewish refugees in the 1930s.

While I cannot presume to know the exact conversations that occurred between travelers, I can readily imagine that information was shared among those seeking an escape from a darkening situation in Europe, especially those identified on passenger lists as "Hebrews."

As I researched the lives of more of Lucia's fellow passengers, I found myself swept up in the events swirling around those people as World War II approached, and as the lives of each one moved through those events. I felt pressured to know what happened to each passenger!

Accountant

On his *World War I Draft Registration Card*, signed August 9, 1917, **Willard Charles Brown**, age twenty-two said he was an accountant for The Seoul Mining Company, in Chosen, Korea. By the 1939 trip to England, forty-four year old Brown was an engineer born in Colorado.

Aviators

Josiah Claramont Towle was a U.S. citizen born on July 19, 1905, who gave his occupation as "Air Pilot" and traveled with his wife **Evelyn Towle** on this spring 1939 voyage. Interestingly they traveled to Scotland in September 1939 – after the fall of Poland – and returned from Glasgow on September 19 aboard the *S.S. Orizaba*, sailing for New York. On the ship's list of passengers, they indicated they had "no occupation." That ship was a transport ship for the U.S. Navy in both World War I and World War II. According to the *1940 US Census*, he lived in Los Angeles and earned $5000+ as a pilot, and had lived in 1935 in Dallas. He was mustered into the U. S. Navy on December 15, 1941, and served aboard the *U.S.S. Albemarle AV-5* as a SealC. The *Albemarle* was one of only two Curtiss-class seaplane tenders built for the United States Navy just prior to the United States' entry into World War II. Named for Albemarle Sound on the North Carolina coast, she was the third U.S. Naval vessel to bear the name, she served in the Caribbean and the Atlantic during World War II.

Bankers

Another "Hebrew" on board was **Alfred Rosenfeld**, born in Germany in 1894, most recently a citizen of Rotterdam, Holland. By 1940 he became the president of a bank in New York according to the *1940 US Census*, New York. He traveled during the 1930s with his wife, **Emmy**: 1936 from England to New York, and in 1937 from Cherbourg, France, to New York. They traveled aboard the *S.S. Normandie* (a sister ship to the *S.S. Nieuw Amsterdam*) arriving in Le Havre, France on April 26, 1939, and left from that port on May 1, 1939, (*New York Passenger Lists, 1820-1957. S.S. Normandie*). That he should turn around and board the *S.S. Nieuw Amsterdam* on May 22, 1939, for its voyage to Southampton is interesting. And again, weeks after the fall of Poland, he and Emmy sailed from New York to Southampton on October 22, 1939, and returned from Rotterdam on October 31, 1939, aboard the *S.S. Statendam* (a sister ship to the *S.S. Nieuw Amsterdam*), giving their last address as Rotterdam, Holland. It appears he took one final trip alone to Europe with a return to New York in November 1939. In 1940, the *S.S. Statendam* (actually, the *S.S. Statendam III* 1929-1940) was scrapped after it had been burned in Rotterdam to avoid capture by the Nazis who invaded Holland on May 10.

As mentioned earlier, the *S.S. Nieuw Amsterdam* was conscripted by the Allies during World War II to transport troops. So too, in the Pacific Theater, was the fate of at least one Japanese cruise liner. **Joseph C. Gillon-Fergusson** and his wife, **Elfrida**, were mentioned earlier as a banker and his wife on holiday from their duties in Shanghai, and who later were interned by the Japanese. Interestingly, it was the *Tatsuta Maru*, a Japanese cruise liner, conscripted in October 1941 for wartime use as a troop carrier by the Imperial Japanese Navy that carried the first European internees in the first prisoner of war exchange in 1942 in the Pacific Theater. As a cruise liner in the 1930s, the *Tatsuta Maru* sailed regularly from Yokohama, Asia, and the west coast of the United States, and Hawaii. It was a vessel built by Mitsubishi Shipbuilding in Nagasaki; her maiden voyage was April 25, 1930. In July 1940 she disembarked forty Jewish refugees from Russia, Austria, Germany, Norway, and Britain. This exercise was repeated in August 1941 with three hundred forty-nine Jewish refugees. That October, the ship arrived in Hawaii and disembarked American nationals returning to the United States due to deteriorating relations between the U.S. and Japan. In November, the *Tatsuta Maru* was the last passenger ship to leave the United States before the start of the war in the Pacific.

In correspondence with the Hong Kong & Shanghai Banking Corporation in England, I received a copy of an interoffice letter from 1942 with a slip attached that read: "Fergusson wife and Hutchinson all well and in comfort. All taking advantage repatriation scheme. Expect to leave Hankow fifth June. Bank completely taken over 16th December. Best Wishes."

The letter itself went on to state:

> I understand that the Americans are leaving Shanghai in a day or two but the British are not scheduled to sail until 23rd July. It seems too good to be true that all our men in the hands of the Japanese will be repatriated but the Foreign Office must have a Priority List which they might show you or, at least, give you information about our Staff. I do not expect the British will get out of Honkong {sic} but there is a chance that they will get out of Manila, where the Americans won't.

I will pass on the above information about Hankow and will ask Muriel to wire you. I am told that the Fergusson children's address is Strathcona Lodge, Shawnigan Lake, Vancouver Island, B. C. I will also ask Muriel to send them a cable telling them the good news.

The above was from personal communication) Matilda B. J. Knowler, Archives Trainee, HSBC Holdings PLC HGHQ. The letters infer that the Fergussons' sailing dates roughly match the *Tatsuta Maru's* departure date from Shanghai to Lourenco Marques. It is likely, then, that the Fergusson family was aboard the *Tatsuta Maru*.

I wondered about the number of Jewish people in Japan, then learned that **Chiune Sugihara**, a Japanese diplomat stationed in Lithuania, rescued some six thousand Jews by signing transit visas for them. With this document, many traveled across Russia to Kobe, Japan, then on to Shanghai, China. When I reviewed the list of people who secured this precious document, I found names of Lithuanian and Polish Jews (from both east and west Poland) along with a smattering of British citizens, Canadians, and one American. The diplomat, assisted by his wife, did this work between July 31 and August 28, 1940, when he was reassigned to another post. He is the only Japanese citizen named on the list of *Righteous among Nations* by the country of Israel.

When the *Tatsuta Maru* sailed with internees in 1942, the trip took several weeks with stops at many Pacific islands. Specifically, she departed Yokohama July 30, 1942, with sixty Allied internees, embarked more at Shanghai, Saigon, and Singapore. She arrived at Lourenco Marques, Portuguese East Africa, on August 27 with nearly one thousand Allied personnel. These people were exchanged with the British for Japanese diplomats and supplies, including 48,818 Red Cross parcels designated for Allied prisoners of war in Japanese custody. On a second such trip to exchange prisoners of war (including six hundred sixty-three Canadians), the *Tatsuta Maru* was torpedoed and sunk by the *U.S.S. Tarpon*, leaving scant survivors.

Businessmen/Entertainment

As I wrote the story of the passengers, I held another question in the back of my mind: Why did several passengers, especially women, identify themselves as actresses, when they were, in fact, stenographers or teachers or librarians?

Then I discovered that **Hal B. Wallis** and his wife, **Louisa F. Wallis**, were aboard the ship on its voyage to Southampton. They traveled with their son, **Hal Brent Wallis**, age five years. The elder Wallis was born Aaron Blum Wolowicz to Polish Ashkenazi Jews. His parents changed their last name to Wallis, and he eventually became known as Harold Blum Wallis when he was born in Chicago September 14, 1898. Later he became known as Harold Brent "Hal B" Wallis. On the trip to England he identified himself as an "Executive," and his wife was listed as a

"Housewife." The *1930 US Census* stated he was an "Associate in moving pictures" and his wife, Louise, was an "Actress in moving pictures." She starred in seventy-one films from 1913 to 1939. When Hal B. Wallis registered for the *World War II Draft*, he revealed he worked for Warner Brothers in Burbank. He was very wealthy, with at least four servants.

Warner Brothers produced *Heart of the North*, shown aboard the *S.S. Nieuw Amsterdam*, having released it on December 10, 1938. Movie reviewers hailed its success as a technicolor wonder and it is now considered a classic for its time. Wallis produced *Casablanca, The Maltese Falcon, Sergeant York*, and *True Grit*, among scores of other films. Future President Ronald Reagan worked for Wallis in two films.

With a major movie producer on board, and the fact that passengers were often given a list of all passengers as a souvenir, it is not a stretch to assume many may have changed their occupations temporarily in the hope of being "discovered," including my Aunt Lucia on her voyage home in August.

Businessmen/General

Ronald Elliot Curtis married **Julia Madeleine Brinkerhoff** in 1903 and enlisted in 1904 in Troop B, Squadron A Cavalry, New York, and served with Troop D, Squadron A, on the Mexican Border in 1916. Commissioned Captain in Ordnance, June 1, 1917, he served at Watervliet Arsenal, with the 42nd Division, General Headquarters A. E. F. Commander Ordnance Division Railway, Artillery Supply Depot. He was promoted to Major May 6, 1919, while serving with the Army of Occupation in Germany. After World War I and his discharge in August 1919 he became a successful real estate broker with Ruland & Benjamin-Earle & Calhoun, Inc. who brokered luxury apartments, among other properties in New York.

The Director of the Spirella Corset Company was also on board. **William E. Hosler**, born in 1873, traveled with his wife and two sons; he stated his occupation was "Manufacturer." The company made women's made-to-measure corsets beginning about 1903. (Apparently corset manufacturing was of singular importance during the early part of the 20th Century. See the vignette about Dr. Ira DeVer Warner and his brother Dr. Lucien Calvin Warner, p. 78. Spirella had subsidiaries in London, Canada, and Germany and designers worked to create corsets that fit the shift in the design of women's fashions, particularly those from Europe. No doubt, Hosler was visiting the London facility. I found the on-line resource most informative, albeit showing tortuous pieces of clothing.

The catalogue stated the following, "In Paris, where style in dress reaches its greatest perfection, the corset is of first importance. No smartly dressed Parisian lady would wear a corset other than one fitted to her individual measurements. One leading Parisian modiste will not design a gown without first designing and fitting the corset upon which the gown is to be worn. One of the world's authorities on fashion has said: 'The secret of being well dressed lies in your figure and your figure is made or ruined by your corset. Don't order your gown until you have bought the right corset.' "

Bronxville Village, New York, was home to **Roy Earl Demmon**, his wife **Elizabeth "Betty"** and their son, **Roy, Jr.**, age thirteen. His occupation was indicated as "Chemicals" on the passenger list. By the *1940 US Census*, Roy, Sr., age forty-nine, was Vice President and Office Manager for a wholesale chemical company. The household employed a maid. He was wealthy enough to send their son to Riverdale Country Day School, then to the exclusive boarding school, The Taft School in Watertown, Connecticut, and on to Yale University and Harvard University. In 1981, Roy, Jr., worked in Washington, D. C. for the Reagan Administration as Executive Assistant to the U. S. Department of Housing and Urban Development, and Director of Operations and Marketing for the Federal Loan Board.

Engineers

Norbert and **Emil Erdreich**, brothers ages thirty-five and thirty-two respectively, were engineers. When each signed the *World War II Draft Registration Card*, they indicted their birth place was Baku, Russia, born of "Hebrew" parents. They immigrated as a family to the United States in November, 1922. Norbert signed his card on February 16, 1942, and sadly died July 31, 1942, at age thirty-eight; his *Draft Registration Card* has a hand-written notation in capital letter DECEASED across the top. When he signed the card, he lived in Washington, DC with his brother and stated he was an unemployed engineer.

The brothers had traveled together in 1933 to England and again in May 1941 to Portugal. I was unable to determine the reasons for these trips. In the *1940 US Census*, Emil Erdreich worked for the Census Bureau in Economics and Statistical Research. His *Draft Registration Card*, signed on October 16, 1940, is more specific: he worked for the Bureau of the Census, Division of Mines and Quarries doing "Domestic and District Research." In fact, Emil was Chief, Program Section (Principal Economist) of the Zinc Division within the Office of Vice Chairman for Metals and Minerals, under the War Production Board within the Executive Office of the President. So, Emil was part of the United States Civil Service Commission and provided a valuable service to the war effort: zinc chromate was a mineral used to create a non-corrosive paint primer applied to the inside of fighters and bombers. Zinc was also used in batteries, essential for war materiel. Further research indicated that lead and zinc were the "gold" of World War II, and that the zinc coins were circulated in Germany and occupied lands between 1940 and 1945.

Intrigued by this specificity, I researched just what and why the Census Bureau tracked the business of mines and quarries. I learned that the Bureau has done so since 1902 when it began compiling data on mines, quarries, petroleum and natural gas wells by states and by territories. Enumeration included iron ore, manganese, lead, copper, gold, and silver, along with coal and clay, and so forth. By 1920, statistics on labor, wages, capital, supplies and materials and other specific economic data also were tabulated. I realized that with Emil's education in engineering, this job suited him very well and the information was useful to a government that, in 1940, was putting itself on a war footing. In 1949, Emil flew in a government-owned aircraft from Frankfurt to Westover AFB, Massachusetts; it is now the largest operational Air Force installation in the United States.

Another engineer was **David Allan Shepard**, thirty-five in 1939, who had lived much of his life in Colorado. In 1930, the Census listed him as a "Chemical engineer, oil refinery." He was a graduate of MIT. By September 19, 1943, however, when he traveled back from Ireland to New York (which had to be a treacherous trip given the Nazi submarine activity), he listed his occupation as "Civil servant" on his passport. He traveled again in October 1944 returning from Scotland to the United States. As I came to understand what individuals were called upon to do during World War II, it seemed reasonable that he would not give a clear answer to that question. He died as a retired chemical engineer.

Lawyers

Walter John Blenko, born March 4, 1899, was a successful attorney with a general practice in 1930. Also, he had a radio and his property was worth $13,000. In World War I, he signed the *World War I Draft Registration Card 1917-1918* on September 27, 1918, and stated he was a machine designer at American University in Washington, D. C. He lived in Ohio, but was a British citizen and served in the United Kingdom's Royal Air Force as an Air Cadet, Short Service for the Duration of the War. He served from September 1918 to April 1919 and was discharged because he was "surplus to R. A.F. requirements (not having suffered impairment); he served 100 days." Naturalized as an American citizen by 1940, Blenko had two servants and he and his family traveled to France in the mid-1930s. By 1940 he worked in Pittsburgh as a private practice attorney. In 1942 he signed the *World War II Draft Registration Card 1942* (Old Man's Draft) stating he worked for Stebbins & Blenko. Notably, he was the son of William J. Blenko, who started the Blenko Glass Company in 1893 in West Virginia; the company continues its business of creating elaborate glassware.

Another wealthy lawyer traveling Tourist Class, was **Joseph C. Wilberding, Jr.**, who specialized in insurance law. He married well: **Katherine van Cortlandt** was the daughter of **Augustus van Cortlandt**, a successful real estate broker. They were married May 20, 1939, one day before the *S.S. Nieuw Amsterdam* sailed for England, so the voyage was the start of their honeymoon. Joseph was born in 1918 and maintained his Manhattan law career until at least 1960; his household included servants.

Medical Personnel

A British physician, **Dr. Bernard Wilfred Goldstone,** was born in 1904 to wealthy Jewish parents who raised him in a household that included servants. His father was a mantle manufacturer, a piece of equipment used to crush stone. This would have been a lucrative business given the large number of stone quarries in England. Bernard served his country during World War II in the Royal Army Medical Corps, 1942-1945, earning the rank of Lieutenant.

The **Hops brothers, Wilfred and Kenneth**, were born in South Africa, and, by 1939, were "Dental Surgeons" having gone to dental school in England. Wilfred lived his life in Nairobi, Kenya, and died in 1956 at age fifty-nine. Kenya was part of the British Empire in 1939.

Richard Hardy Appel was a physician, age thirty-seven, traveling Third Class on this trip, having received his medical degree from Butler University, Indianapolis, in 1921. He was a "Medical specialist" according to the *1940 US Census.* In July, 1939 he sailed back to New York from Glasgow, Scotland, so, for this trip to England, he stayed about six to seven weeks. He traveled alone presumably because his wife was pregnant with their first child, who was born in August. Significantly, he served his country as a Naval Reserve Officer moving in rank from Lt. Commander to Commander to Captain between 1942 and about 1984 as stated in the *United States Select Military Register 1862-1985.*

Merchants

The story of another Jewish man was very intriguing, albeit horrifying. He was the first passenger listed in Cabin Class: **Joseph Asscher**, twenty-six, born December 12, 1912, Dutch, and a diamond dealer, who lived in Amsterdam, Holland. He traveled extensively in the 1930s between Europe and the United States. Records of his travels ended with the *S. S. Nieuw Amsterdam* voyage to Rotterdam from Southampton in late May 1939.

A review of myriad on-line entries about the history of the Holocaust and World War II revealed that Abraham Asscher (Joseph's grandfather or great uncle) founded the Asscher Diamond Company (now the Royal Asscher Diamond Company) in 1854. He and his brother Joseph built its international fame, especially when they cleaved the legendary Cullinan Diamond, the largest rough gem-quality diamond ever found. There were six elder Asscher brothers involved in the company.

Abraham Asscher was a leader in the Dutch-Jewish community. When the Nazi *Wehrmacht* invaded the Netherlands, it surrendered to the Nazis in May 1940. The entire Asscher family and the firm's 500 gem polishers were interred in concentration camps, with seven, at least, interred in Bergen-Belsen, a notorious death camp, on September 15, 1944. From April 7 to April 13, 1945, they were taken by train to Westerbork Transit Camp from Bergen-Belsen, to Farsleben. En route, the train was liberated by the 743rd Tank Battalion of the 30th Infantry Division as described in the *Passenger List of the Death Train (Destined for Theresienstadt) Bergen-Belsen to Farsleben, Germany.*

On the list of survivors are only seven members of the Asscher family that I could identify by that surname (ten reportedly survived, but, presumably, these last three were using different surnames), including Joseph Asscher, and only fifteen of the original five hundred gem polishers. The record confirms that the younger Joseph Asscher was liberated on April 13, 1945. One year later on March 21, 1946, he traveled from Amsterdam as a diamond dealer to the United States.

Another extremely successful man was **Hugo Robert Lehrfeld**, born in New York on July 27, 1885, to parents who emigrated from Germany. Early in his career he was a merchant for a smelting refinery that dealt in precious metals. The Kastenhuber and Lehrfeld Company of New York was a refinery of precious metals (gold, silver, and platinum) from at least 1915 through the 1950s. Lehrfeld traveled extensively on behalf of the company from the 1920s through at least 1948 initially as a smelter, then as a buyer for the company, and eventually as its president. His work took him many times to Cuba, England, and Europe. A wealthy concern, the company was awarded a patent in 1930 for an alloy for a pen point.

A Russian-born Jewish man was one of several furriers listed on board the ship. By the *1940 US Census*, **Robert Ehrmann**, born in 1895 in Kazan, was an executive in the fur industry, and had lived in Berlin until October 1938 when he sailed Cabin Class to the United States via England. He spoke English, German, and Russian. He gave his permanent address as Berlin when he sailed aboard the *SS Nieuw Amsterdam* on this trip. Interestingly, a hand-written note on the passenger list indicated he had "medical certification for defective vision." No specification was given and I noted at least one other passenger with that notation, signed by the ship's doctor.

The Nazi paramilitary wing in Germany launched *Kristallnacht* (the Night of Broken Glass) on November 8-9, 1938. This was an orchestrated attack against all Jewish-owned businesses or places of worship throughout Germany.

Erhmann's wife, **Alexandra**, was in Berlin until March 24, 1939, when she sailed to New York, and was listed as a "Hebrew" with a permanent address in Berlin. She must have returned to England and perhaps to Germany sometime between April and October 1939 because her last trip to New York from Southampton was November 6, 1939. On the passenger list under the column "Nationality or country of which citizen subject" the word "Without" was typed. How very sad for her; she then gave her permanent address as New York.

Bennie Cassel, thirty-nine, cotton or textile manufacturer/merchant, came into the United States on April 22, 1939. Born in Odessa, Russia, he was Jewish according to the *1911 England Census*, and came from a family of textile workers. He had been a merchant seaman in the British armed forces during World War I. He traveled extensively by ship in the 1930s and again in 1940; this latter year was particularly dangerous as Nazi submarines dominated the Atlantic by then.

Bertram Anthony Wine, thirty-one, was born March 10, 1908, in Northern Ireland near Belfast and was an antique dealer, and a British citizen. On the passenger manifest under the column "Race or people" he indicated "Hebrew." On other trips, he identified himself as "English." When he traveled from Liverpool to New York in March 1945 he listed his occupation as "Silver specialist" and a trip from Southampton to New York in December 1945 he was again an "Antique dealer." At his passing, on January 19, 1981, he left a very large estate.

Alfred Disraeli Webber, thirty-three, born June 3, 1909. This Jewish family immigrated to England from Austro-Hungary and were naturalized British citizens in 1906. Alfred became a merchant/company director and traveled the Pacific and the Atlantic on business in 1935, including a trip to the Philippines and a temporary visit in Tokyo as described on the *List or Manifest of Alien Passengers for the United States, March 4, 1935*. He was an industrialist who co-owned Pifco Safety Wireglobe Company with his brother presumably until their deaths in the 1980s. The *1939 Register* confirms that Alfred D. Webber was single and a general manager for a wholesale electrical distribution company. The *England and Wales Death Registration Index 1837-2007*, lists his death as 1983 in Manchester.

Another merchant was **LeRoy Miller Morris,** who at age fifty-five in 1939, had been a bookstore owner since at least 1910 in California as indicated in the *1910 US Census*. I could find no other data on this hard working man.

The occupation "Colonial engineer sugar technologist' was interesting. **Cornelius Joamner Hugo Penning**, age fifty-two and an experienced sugar merchant traveling from 1918 through at least 1946 to Hawaii, to India, and the Philippine Islands, and to Cuba and the Canal Zone, to name a few ports of call. He was Dutch-born, but lived in England. Hawaii was a major sugar producer as were the other countries named above. Sugar was the first food item to be rationed during the war. The Japanese controlled the Philippine Islands and cargo from Hawaii and the Caribbean had to be curtailed because ships were diverted for war purposes. Also there were heavy losses in 1942 from the sinking of cargo ships by the Nazi U-boats.

A Chicago general manager of a printing company, **Edward Oatman Vandercook**, age forty-one, was a leader in the printing press business. He began to work for his father who founded Vandercook Press, after his stint in the United States Navy in World War I. The elder Vandercook had invented the proof press and his sons managed the company until it was sold in 1968.

Military Intelligence

The occupational category of "military intelligence" is one that I surmised. Likely, many of the well-educated, politically astute and successful business people, and scientists on board the *S.S. Nieuw Amsterdam* were recruited by the Allies to serve the war effort. I identified the following passenger as likely heavily involved in the war.

Graham Eyres-Monsell's full name was **Henry Bolton Graham Eyres-Monsell, 2nd Viscount Monsell.** He was born November 21, 1905, and by age thirty-three, identified his occupation as "Research." In fact, Eyres-Monsell was part of British Intelligence Corps during World War II and earned the rank of Lt. Colonel. He helped plan *Operation Torch*, a British/United States invasion of French North Africa during the North African Campaign of November 1942. He was cited for meritorious action in the face of the enemy. This man's actions had a direct bearing on the life of Aunt Lucia's youngest brother, William Arthur Payton, age eighteen, who was mustered in to the United States Navy October 31, 1942, and boarded the *USS Samuel Chase.* The *Samuel Chase* served as a flagship for the landings at Algiers, part of the Allied invasion of North Africa on November 8, 1942. Samuel Chase was a signatory to the United States Declaration of Independence.

Philanthropists

Another passenger, **John Moore Kelso Davis II**, born August 18, 1908, became a civic leader in Connecticut renowned for his serving as a board member of many philanthropic, regulatory, and historical organizations such as serving as the President of the Connecticut Historical Society. He served in World War II as a Second Lieutenant of Field Artillery in the Officers Reserve Corp. He retired as a Lt. Colonel with a Bronze Star and *La Medaille de Reconnaissance, francaise* for his service in the European Theater. His occupation on the 1939 passenger list was "Printer." From 1952 to 1973 he was the President of Case, Lockwood & Brainerd Company, later Connecticut Printers, Inc., a company for which his father was president. His family was extremely wealthy; his father's home was valued at $86,000 in 1930.

Professors

The information on **Ralph Eugene Root, PhD.** is excerpted from his lengthy obituary. Senior Professor Emeritus of the United States Naval Postgraduate School, Annapolis, Maryland, died September 23, 1961, in Franklin, New Hampshire, near his summer home in Sanbornton, at the age of eighty-two years.

Ralph Eugene Root was born in July 1879, in Trenton, Missouri, and attended Morningside College in Sioux City, Iowa, and earned the Sc.B. degree in Mathematics in 1905. He received the M.Sc. degree in 1909 from the University of Iowa, then studied at the University of Chicago under the eminent mathematician E. H. Moore and received his Ph.D. in Mathematics, Summa cum Laude, in 1911. Professor Root's doctoral dissertation, *Iterated Limits in General Analysis*, is still in use as one of the fundamental reference works for mathematics.

Ralph Root married in December 1904 to **Mary Keziah Batcheller**. Root was a mathematics instructor from 1906 to 1910 at the University of Iowa. From 1911 to 1913 he taught at the University of Missouri. In 1913 he taught at the United States Naval Academy in Annapolis as Professor of Mathematics and Mechanics. When the Naval Postgraduate School (NPS) was created at Annapolis in 1914, Root became the first civilian professor in the Postgraduate School. When the NPS restarted after World War I, Root served as Head of the Department of Mathematics and Mechanics from 1919 to 1946. Morningside College of Sioux City, Iowa, awarded an honorary Sc.D. degree to him in 1942. Root retired from teaching in 1946 with the title Emeritus, the first professor in any of the service schools so named. In addition to his textbooks and scientific writing, Root authored a historical novel, *The Prairie Pebble*, based on his personal experiences growing up on the American prairie in the late 19th Century.

In 1939, **Joseph Henry Willits, PhD,** said he was an "Economist," and was Dean and Professor of Economics at the Wharton School, Westchester, New York. He was born in June 1889, as a Hixite Friend (Quaker), a sect within the Friends' organization. During World War I Willits was the employment manager for a United States Navy aircraft factory. He had registered for the World War I Draft on June 4, 1917, but claimed an exemption because he was the sole support for his wife and child. He was age twenty-eight and an instructor at the University of Pennsylvania. He had been a teacher at Swarthmore College, Pennsylvania in 1920, then a university teacher in 1930. During World War II, he signed the *World War II Draft Registration Card 1942* (Old Man's Draft); he was age fifty-two and had worked for the Rockefeller Foundation since 1939 as Director of the Division of Social Sciences. Likely as a result of his Quaker upbringing, Willits guided its programs through the war years and led the division toward greater support for work in international relations and area studies.

Religious Leaders/Relief Workers

Born in Vienna, Austria, in 1871 to American parents, **Henry Copley Greene** was an "Editor" in 1939 aboard the *S.S. Nieuw Amsterdam*. He lived in France from 1917 to 1920 and returned to the United States in 1922 with his daughter. In 1916, Greene worked for the Massachusetts Commission for the Blind, Boston, founded by Helen Keller, and did relief work in England and France. In 1922 he completed a series of health talks for the American Red Cross and Boston Department of Health Services. In 1898, he was a noted author of *Theophile: A Miracle Play*, and in 1905, he wrote *The Father: A Drama*, and he wrote *The Children's Crusade* among other religious writings. His books and plays are considered classics. In his lifetime, he was an author, translator, editor, publisher, and contributor.

An 1894 graduate of Harvard University, Henry C. Greene, along with his wife **Rosaline Huidekoper** and daughter, **Katrine**, were heavily involved in war relief work during both world wars. Officially, he was a "Clerk, Boston Art Museum" according to the *1940 US Census*. He volunteered for the American Red Cross and the Unitarian Service Committee. In May 1940 the Unitarian Service Committee (USC) was established as a standing committee of the American Unitarian Association. Its focus was on finding opportunities for humanitarian service in America and abroad. It aided displaced person in occupied areas, finding passage for many to the United States. USC exists today with the same purpose.

It stands to reason that the Greene family knew of the seminal theological work done by **John Hassler Dietrich**, whose vignette appears in *Afterword Part II*, page 84. And likely they knew about the work assigned by the Wellesley, Massachusetts, Unitarian Church to the Reverend Waitstill Hastings Sharp and his wife Martha Sharp, in February 1939, to go to Prague, Czechoslovakia, to save hundreds of imperiled dissidents and Jewish refugees as depicted in *Defying the Nazis: The Sharps' War*, both a PBS documentary, and a book. The country fell to the Nazis in March 1939.

Scientists

Elias Avery Lowe, born to Jewish parents in Moscow, immigrated to the United States in 1889, where he met **Helen Tracy Porter**, a Pennsylvania-born woman; they married in 1911. They lived in Europe in the early 1900s where he received his doctorate at the University of Munich in 1908. They were in residence at Oxford during the 1930s and in residence again after World War II when he applied to return to England "to continue my interrupted sources of lectures in Oxford and to continue my paleographical research" as stated on his July 25, 1919, Passport Application. Among the Lowes' descendants are English artist Charlotte Johnson Wahl, and her son, journalist and politician Boris Johnson, former Mayor of London and the former Secretary of State for Foreign and Commonwealth Affairs.

Lowe was a faculty member of the prestigious Institute for Advanced Studies, School of History, from 1936 to 1945. The Institute was founded in reaction to the rise of Fascism, so it became a lifeline in the migration of European scholars to the United States. Notably, the Institute accepted women students as opposed to other graduate schools in the 1930s. Past faculty have included Albert Einstein, one of its first Professors who remained at the Institute until his death in 1955, and distinguished scientists and scholars such as Kurt Gödel, J. Robert Oppenheimer, Erwin Panofsky, Hetty Goldman, Homer A. Thompson, John von Neumann, George Kennan, Hermann Weyl, and Clifford Geertz. Among his myriad honors over his lifetime, Lowe was a Consultant to the Library of Congress. See page 71 for a brief vignette about **H. T. Lowe-Porter**, his wife.

Teachers

Similarly, **David L. McKaye**, a forty-nine-year old teacher traveled with his wife **Julia G. McKaye** to England in May 1939 and to Norway in November, returning to the Port of New York December 1. He was with the Department of Adult Education in San Jose, California. The start of the Nazis occupation of Norway did not occur until April 1940 eight months after the invasion of Poland. However, travelers to Norway during that time must have been wary.

Writers

Both voyages had writers on board, including **Harry Frederick Kern, Jr.**, who wrote for *Newsweek* and traveled extensively to Europe and Japan in the 1950s as an "Editor." Harvard educated, 1930-1935, he joined *Newsweek* in 1935 and became assistant editor in 1937, then associate editor by 1941. During World War II, he was the war editor. In the 1950s he moved from senior editor of international affairs for *Newsweek* magazine, New York City, 1950-1956 and became editor-in-chief of international edits, and, finally, president of Foreign Reports, 1956. He was a Member, Council on Foreign Relations, a leading foreign policy organization. The Japanese government awarded him the Order of Sacred Treasure Japan, and he received the Order of Merit (Lebanon), both presumably for his international work after World War II.

Women on board the May 1939 Voyage

When I analyzed the occupations of the passengers for both voyages, married women were commonly identified as "Housewife" and I found an inordinate number of women with that designation. Any other occupation identified by women stood out by comparison, and further seemed to imply the woman was unmarried. Other occupations for women were "Nurse," "Maid," "Teacher," "Secretary," "Stenographer," "Mannequin," or "Actress." Information on some women was difficult or impossible to trace, especially if they traveled alone or if they had a very common surname. Without the corroborating name of a spouse, child, parent or sibling I could not triangulate information about some of the women, so they were left out of the telling.

First, there is a mystery about Aunt Lucia's cabin mate on the trip to England. Lucia indicated in Letter 2 that her cabin mate was a "doctor from Austria." I found no women doctors from Austria. As mentioned above, I found only one woman from Austria, and she was listed in "Cabin Class." This was **Rosa Kuschei** (Rosina Kuschei) born on October 2, 1901, making her age thirty-eight, rather than twenty-seven, the age listed on the passenger manifest. Later documents corroborate her age and date of birth in 1901. She was a "Ladies Maid" for her entire career, and traveled with her "friend," Mrs. W. Grant. In fact, Kuschei traveled with Mrs. Grant in 1937 and 1938 to England always as a "Ladies Maid" and always in Cabin Class. Gertrude Grant, age fifty-two in 1939, was the wife of William W. Grant, Jr., a successful lawyer in Denver, Colorado. Rosina, a naturalized American citizen, spent her adult life in Colorado, but made several visits to Innsbruk, Austria, after the end of World War II.

Journalists

A divorced journalist, **Elise Fritz** was born in Germany about 1895, and traveled in Europe in the 1930s, spoke German and identified herself on one voyage as a "Photographer." Her name is a common one, and without knowing if Fritz was her own family name or her married name, I was unable to find more information about her.

Merchants

Caroline Pauline deVries was a Brazilian citizen, who was born in Guyana about 1897 and spoke Dutch, and was of the "Portuguese race." She indicated in 1939 that she was a "Timber merchant," but on other voyages her occupation was "Housewife" or "None." The export of timber was, and continues to be, a major economic resource for Brazil.

No Occupation/Housewife

Helen L. Leveson, whose full name was Helen Frances L. Leveson died at age seventy-eight in 1980. She was married to Barnett Leveson, a very successful furrier, if the number and extent of the trips she took in the 1930s, in 1940, and again after the end of World War II, are any evidence. She and Barnett were "Hebrews" – he from England and she from the United States.

Helen Liflander Leveson was in her late 30s when she traveled with her twin daughters **Nona Liflander Leveson** and **Barbara Liflander Levesen**, aged two years. They traveled Tourist Class, but his name appeared on the Alien List because he was a British citizen arriving at the Port of New York. Because their father, **Barnett Levesen**, a wealthy furrier, was British, the girls held dual citizenship, according to the Consular Report of the Birth for 1937. Helen and her husband sailed to England at least twice in the early 1930s. Helen took her daughters to Ireland in June 1940. This latter trip had to have been an extreme act of faith as the Battle of the Atlantic between the Allies and Axis navies and air forces ran from 1939 to the end of the war, and Italy had entered the war on June 10, 1940. Of particular concern in the Atlantic was the activity of the German U-boats which had sunk the cruise liner *Athenia* off the coast of Ireland in 1939.

The **Schoonmaker twins, Beatrice and Muriel**, were born in New York on January 26, 1915. They traveled extensively with their parents in the 1930s, and listed no occupation for themselves. In 1937 and in 1940 they went to Bermuda; again citing no occupation and by now in their mid-twenties. Their father, Jacob Schoonmaker, was a dealer in wholesale notions, and died in 1943 at the age of eighty-eight. Presumably, they had no need for an occupation.

When **Madeleine Curtis (Julia Madeleine)** went to England in May, she gave no occupation for herself, but when she left in June 1939 she identified herself as a fifty-six year old "Travel Agent." As the wife of **Ronald Elliot Curtis**, she had traveled extensively to the West Indies, Bermuda, England, and Europe. In 1921 she registered as an American citizen in Geneva for the "education of children" and stayed for one year with her four daughters, ages eight, sixteen, and twins at age eighteen according to their Application for Registration – American Citizen, May 18, 1921. That she and her daughters could afford this luxury in their education is reflective of her husband's apparent success as a broker in New York real estate. From 1910 through the 1930s, the Curtis household included two to four servants, both English and French. Remarks for Ronald Elliot Curtis are on page 59.

Married to **Carl Freeland Eveleigh, Anna Sneed Megee Eveleigh** traveled Cabin Class in 1939. Her husband was an "Executive, machine manufacturing" according to the *1940 US Census*. However, his *World War I Draft Registration 1917-1918*, signed June 5, 1917, stated he was an accountant for Eli Lilly. This was corroborated by his signing the *World War II Draft Registration Card 1942* (Old Man's Draft) in 1942, which stated he worked for Eli Lilly and Company. He was successful working at this large pharmaceutical company, and his household employed two servants in 1940.

Teachers

The **Parker sisters, Anita Mae and Lois Virginia**, were seasoned travelers in the 1930s, sailing to Europe and to Shanghai, China, and returned to Honolulu in 1935, coincidentally aboard the Japanese cruise liner, the *Tatsuta Maru* (see the story of the Fergusson family on page 57-58. They identified themselves as teachers. By May 1939, on the trip to England, Anita stated she was a "Stenographer," and Lois a "Secretary," but when they returned to the United States in August, they had morphed into teachers again.

Writers

Identifying herself as a "Writer," Helga Iversen was a twenty-eight-year old Californian who wrote for *Sunset Magazine*, San Francisco, a popular publication that covered myriad travel news, and is still in print. She made an extended trip to Europe between May and July 1939.

Another writer, **Helen Tracy Porter Lowe,** used her skills - "Secretary to husband" - to translate for her husband **Elias Avery Lowe** (originally spelled Loew), a noted Oxford scholar and paleography researcher. As a translator, she was known as H. T. Lowe-Porter. For more than two decades, Lowe-Porter enjoyed exclusive rights to translate the works of Thomas Mann from German into English. She was granted these rights in 1925 by Alfred A. Knopf Publishers. She translated Mann's works from 1924 to 1960, and for decades, Lowe-Porter's translations were the only ones that existed in the English-speaking world. See page 67-68 for remarks about her husband.

AFTERWORD PART II

Men aboard the *S.S. Nieuw Amsterdam* on its return voyage to New York in August 1939.

Unless otherwise indicated, all data for the passengers was taken from *Names and Description of ALIEN Passengers, S.S. Nieuw Amsterdam*, leaving the Port of New York, arrived Port of Plymouth, England, 29th May, 1939, or from *Names and Description of ALIEN Passengers Embarked at the Port of Southampton, S.S. Nieuw Amsterdam*, 4th August, 1939. Passenger lists recorded information in many different ways, depending on the individual passenger's on-board accommodations (Cabin, Tourist, Third), whether a passenger was a citizen of the county to which s/he was headed, or if the passenger were an "Alien" to that country, or if the passenger were on a Quota Visa list. Each list provided different types of information.

There were many well educated passengers on this return trip with Aunt Lucia, who had only a high school diploma. I am sure she was aware of the disparity in education between other passengers and herself. As I researched the list, I found women who had attended Lawrence College, University of Wisconsin, and Vassar, as well as men and women who had attended schools of medicine, schools of law, and one who was a Rhodes Scholar. A quick review of passengers' occupations (summarized here for both voyages) elicited these approximations: 113 "Housewives," 38 "Merchants," 13 "Doctors," 14 "Nurses," 9 "Lawyers," 61 "Students," 56 "No occupation," 10 "Retired," 8 "Actors/Actresses," and 4 "Aviators" among fewer numbers of teachers, authors, scientists, bookkeepers, secretaries, stenographers, clerks, and so forth.

Several passengers returning to the United States that August gave peculiar, or false, responses to the question about their occupation. Aunt Lucia stated she was an "Actress" although she was actually a telephone operator. Perhaps she learned from her interactions with Cabin and Tourist Class passengers on the trip to England that being a high school-educated "Teloperator" did not measure up to the occupations and social standing of her fellow passengers. In that vein, on her return trip to the United States, she became very much an actress. Why any passenger would fabricate an occupation is anyone's guess, but reasons could vary from simply being tired of giving the information to trying to hide for personal or political reasons to the hope that networking would provide personal, economic, or social advantages.

The passengers on the return voyage of the *Nieuw Amsterdam* made up a microcosm – their lives were about to be affected by the upcoming war - impacting them in a way that no one individual could have anticipated. World War II, for many of these passengers, created far-reaching changes in their personal lives and professional careers that played a role in world affairs long after the battles ended.

Aviators

Helge W. Anderson, born in Sweden on August 25, 1902, became a naturalized American citizen in January 1925. He did not serve in the American military, and apparently did not serve during World War II. He was a merchant seaman his whole life, married in 1954 and lived in San Francisco as stated in the *1930 Census of Merchant Seamen. The Shipowners and Merchants Tugboat Company, San Francisco.* He served aboard the *Richmond.* He identified himself as an "Aviator" as noted on National Archives for the United Kingdom.

Two men who identified themselves as "Aviator" worked for Lockheed and stated their address was "London." **Perry Goldsmith Hutton** registered for the draft on September 12, 1918, at age 18, giving his birthdate as January 16, 1900, on the *U. S. World War I Draft Registration Cards, 1917-1918.* It is not clear if he served in this war. In 1933, he was living in Peking, China and applied to the Masonic Order through its international lodge in Shanghai. He did this on April 6, 1933, and identified himself as an aviator on his application for the Massachusetts, Mason Membership Cards, 1733-1990. Interestingly, it was noted in the comment section, his application was "put off for further investigation."

The British build-up for war involved American contractors very early on. In January 1939 Perry Hutton entered England to work at Coron Speke Airport (also known as Speke Aeordrome), Liverpool, to work at the Lockheed facility, and in August 1939 returned to the United States aboard the *S.S. Nieuw Amsterdam.* Lockheed's Hudson was an aircraft that served as the backbone for the Royal Air Force (RAF) Costal Command during World War II. The first of this aircraft (Serial #7026) arrived in Liverpool in February 1939, and entered the RAF service in May when the airport was fully militarized. Lockheed was contracted to build and deliver 250 such aircraft by Christmas, 1939.

Gilbert Lawrence Peakes was the second "Aviator" although it seems not officially an aviator. He was a graduate of MIT, an electrical engineer, who worked for Bakelite Corporation in New Jersey for most of his career. His World War I Draft Registration Card reflects this occupation. When he signed the *World War II US Draft Registration Card* (Old Man's Draft), he was age forty-nine and Department Head for Bakelite. The product, Bakelite, was an early plastic used to coat electrical wiring as it is known for its non-conductivity for use in radios and telephones and early machine guns. Pilots' goggles and field telephones used in World War II contained Bakelite. It was also used for wartime patriotic jewelry. There is a Bakelite Museum in Somerset, England.

Bankers

William James McGreal traveled with his wife, noted author **Mary Elizabeth Yates**, who used her family name as a pen name; her vignette is on page 93. They married in England at the US Consulate in December 1929; this was his second marriage according to the *US Consular Reports of Marriages, 1910-1949*. In 1939, McGreal was a banker in New Hampshire, and later moved to New York. Born on July 29, 1888, he was too old to serve in the military, but he signed the *US World War II Draft Registration Cards 1942* (Old Man's Draft) on April 26, 1942. He lived in New Hampshire, was fifty-three years old, and retired. The Old Man's Draft was instituted so that the United States government could assess the skills of it citizenry, with a view to its needs on the home front.

Interestingly, McGreal registered for World War I, citing his occupation as an employee of McGreal Brothers Company, wholesale liquors, a company started by his father of Irish immigrant parentage, in 1905 in Rochester, New York (Gibson's Whiskey). He claimed an exemption because he was "dependent and physical." He had served three years as a "non-com" in the New York National Guard. He stated he was single, age twenty-nine according to the *World War I Draft Registration Cards, 1917-1918*.

Businessmen/General

Abraham Fingerhut, born October 18, 1899, was a successful owner of a millenary business, after a stint as an accountant. He registered for World War I *(World War I Draft Registration Cards, 1917-1918)* signing on September 12, 1918. He traveled extensively from the 1920s through the 1950s, each time associating himself with the millenary business - except for this 1939 voyage, when he identified himself as an "Engineer." By 1940, he was an executive in the millenary trimming business and employed a servant.

One interesting man, a "Tailor" or "Costumer" traveled first class aboard the *Nieuw Amsterdam* in Cabin Class and was listed as a "Visitor" to the United States. By the 1950s had become a "Company director" and worked in textile manufacturing in 1949, at least. He traveled after World War II to South Africa, New Zealand, and Yokohama and sailed the South Atlantic on a cruise. **Henri (also, Henry) Herbert Silbert** was born December 10, 1888, and clearly was a successful businessman; his *World War II US Draft Registration Card 1942* indicated he was "self-employed." He signed the card April 27, 1942, at the age of fifty-four, so this was the Old Man's Draft.

The Bata Shoe Company, Belcamp, Maryland, was started by refugees from Czechoslovakia around the 1930s and was the main employer for the area for many years, with a high of 3000 employees at one time. They made boots for the U. S. Army among other footwear. **Ludvik Gerbec** and his wife **Jana Mencik**, were both born in Czecho-slovakia in the early 1900s and were listed on the Quota Visa tabulation for this August trip to the United States. On his *World War II Draft Registration Card*, the twenty-eight year old Ludvik stated he worked for the Bata Shoe Company. Bata was a two thousand two-hundred acre complex which included a five-story factory, a movie theatre, a hotel, and seventy houses. Historic photographs of this major employer may be found on line. During World War II the hotel was occupied by government employees from Aberdeen Proving Ground, Aberdeen, Maryland. The APG is the Army's oldest active proving ground where the design and testing of ordnance materiel took place.

Although the *1940 US Census* gave no occupation for the Berlin-born **Harold Rose**, a "Hebrew" merchant, he had lived in California since 1935. He signed the *World War II Draft Registration Card* on October 16, 1940, and stated he was employed by Denthol Company in San Francisco; he was twenty-six years old and married.

The son of a British fishmonger, **Sidney Franklyn Cooper,** was a thirty-three year old sugar broker. His job took him on a fairly regular route from Liverpool and Southampton to New York from 1929 through 1939, at least.

Another successful businessman was **Adam Hipolet Kulikowski,** born in Vilna, Poland, on August 22, 1889. In his seventy-seven years he became a naturalized American citizen, traveled extensively to Canada and Europe in the 1930s, then again after World War II to Europe, up to 1960. He signed the *World War II Draft Registration Card 1942* (Old Man's Draft) at the age of fifty-one. He owned the Opportunity Publishing Company, Chicago, Illinois, that published magazines. He owned Ennscorthy Farm in Albemarle County, Virginia, which has been nominated for inclusion on the National Registry of Historic Places.

Cornelius van Abshoven was a Dutch immigrant to the United States. He traveled extensively in the 1930s and 1950s while working as a nurseryman in Watcom County, Washington. The area is well-known for its tulip growing businesses, many of which were established by Dutch immigrants after World War II.

A Russian-born "Hebrew," **Jules Gourary** was a "Company Director" by 1939. His name was on the ship's Quota Immigrant list with his wife, **Regina,** born in Poland, and their son, **Paul**, a student in 1939, born in Germany. They were berthed in Cabin Class. The elder Gourarys were naturalized on December 27, 1944, in the U.S. District Court, New York. Jules signed the (Old Man's) *World War II Draft Registration Card 1942* on April 27 and retired at the age of fifty-nine. Interestingly, **Paul A. Gourary** did not petition for naturalization until January 28, 1957.

Although he said he was retired in 1939 at the age of sixty-five, **Russel E. Palmer** had moved his career forward from grocery clerk in Minneapolis in 1910. Included on the passenger lists for his travel in the 1920s and 1930s to England, he stated he was employed as a "Stationary engineer" in Minneapolis. His 1923 Passport Application said he worked as an "Analyst" for Naphen & Company on Wall Street, New York City, where he lived at the Vanderbilt Hotel.

Paul Renshaw indicated he was a fifty-year old "Professor" returning to New York in 1939. However, according to the *1920 US Census* for Manhattan, he manufactured railway supplies and employed two maids in his home. By the *1930 US Census*, he was "Vice president, factory" and lived on Park Avenue in Manhattan and had increased his home-based employees to four. The *1925 New York State Census* revealed he was a "Railroad engineer," and married, with three servants. By 1947, he lived in New Canaan, Connecticut, and was an executive. On the *World War II Draft Registration Card 1942*, he said he worked for the General Railway Signal Company, Connecticut, and had worked there at least since 1920. Why he said he was a "Professor" on the 1939 trip is unknown.

General Railway Signal Company was established in 1904 and clients for its equipment included major railway lines in the United States. The company's intent was to diversify into areas other than railway signaling. The company's equipment was designed to carry cargo over U. S. rail lines faster and more reliably. It remains a leader in transportation supply to this day. Given the number of companies needed to place the country on a war footing, perhaps Renshaw wanted to deflect conversation away from his real occupation while he sailed from England to New York.

Businessmen/Entertainment

Although **Samuel C. Whiteside**, Corvalis, Oregon, born 1879, stated he was "Retired" in 1939, he and his brother had opened a theater in 1922, and the *1940 US Census* states Whiteside was a "Theater operator." They were the first to offer an evening's entertainment of vaudeville acts, dancing, and silent film to the people of Corvalis, and already operated multiple theaters in the area. Whiteside Theater was later listed on the National Register of Historic Places, renowned for its Italian Renaissance style and the art deco light fixtures. It was owned for sixty-three years by the Whiteside family and now provides a venue for events and entertainment.

Abraham Louis Oppenheim, a British citizen in 1939, traveled Cabin Class as a "Visitor" to the United States. He identified himself as a "Hebrew" born in Russia in 1887. From 1939 through 1960, he identified himself as a "Director" or "Company Director" or "Executive." He traveled with his family extensively to England after World War II and maintained a residence in Beverly Hills, California, from at least 1939. On the *World War II Draft Registration Card 1942* he was fifty-five, so this was the Old Man's Draft with which he complied. He stated he was a British subject by naturalization, but was born in Russia. He signed the document on April 25, 1942.

In 1919 **George Ivan Rosenthal** established a business in moving pictures and represented various manufacturers in the British West Indies, according to his passport application. A May 5, 1920, passport application identified him as being in the moving picture industry. He had actually begun his moving picture business as early as 1915 when he and his wife, **Jennie**, traveled to Jamaica. On the *World War I Draft Registration Card,* signed September 12, 1918, he said he was a merchant in business for himself; he lived in Brooklyn. After World War I, he worked for Arkell and Douglas, Inc., Shipping and Commission Merchants, in the import/export business. The company did business globally (South America, Asia, and the Pacific) including these places Rosenthal traveled: New York, Cape Town, and Trinidad. By 1939, he was successful enough to travel Cabin Class and was considered a "Visitor" to the United States.

Similarly, **Joachim H. Huth**, a German writer naturalized in November 1944 lived in Hollywood and in 1941 described himself as a playwright. Traveling Cabin Class in 1939, he identified himself as such in his travels also in 1937 and again in 1941. He traveled to Cuba in 1941 and to France in 1952. I could find no other information about this man.

Civil Servants

Noted for its exceptional service to its citizens, the British postal service employed **Ernest James Bitten**, who was successful enough to travel Tourist Class. He started with the General Postal Service in 1924 as a "Sorter" but referred to himself as a "Civil Servant" in each ship voyage he took in the 1920s as well as this 1939 trip. Interestingly, there existed a GPO Special Investigations Unit, whose staff intercepted the mail ("postal interception") as part of British intelligence service operations. Whether Bitten was involved in these activities is unknown.

Engineers

On this return trip to the United States, **Howard White Starr**, seventy-six and retired, traveled with his second wife, **Susan,** and their youngest child, **Louis Starr,** age twenty-one. He had four Irish servants in the home in 1940 and he died in November 1946. Howard was successful, but was widowed by 1920, had at least five children at home in 1930 – his home was worth $110,000 - an astonishing value during the Depression. He was a metals engineer and also was referred to as an electrical engineer in Schenectady, New York, on his 1905 Passport Application. Later information elaborates this to his having graduated from Yale University in 1895 and the Stevens Institute in 1900. He was a mechanical engineer in the Street Railway Department, for General Electric Company, Schenectady, New York.

Lawyers

The return trip to New York included notable others such as **Stafford Lofthouse Sands** who was born September 23, 1913, was an attorney and former Finance Minister of the Bahamas, who helped create the tourism industry of that island nation.

One passenger, **Llewellyn John Moses** stated he was a "Jockey" but, in fact, the *1930 US Census* states he was Deputy District Attorney from 1928-1933. According to his obituary, he became a noted defense attorney after that. During World War II, was assigned to the U. S. Attorney's Office in Los Angeles. He signed the *World War II Draft Registration Card* at the age of forty-two and stated he was an attorney at law in private practice. He attended the University of Minnesota, and USC Law School, data which differs from the the *World War I Draft Registration Card A-143* he signed on September 12, 1918, and identified himself as a student at Stanford University, born on September 11, 1899. According to that document, he was "medium tall" and had a slender build with brown eyes and red hair. There were no other physical disabilities cited. I rather doubt he could have been a jockey, based on this description.

Medical Personnel

Other interesting passengers included **Dr. Ira DeVer Warner** and his brother **Dr. Lucien Calvin Warner** who pioneered the "health corset" made of flexible fabric and popular for its light weight material allowing women greater ease of movement: Dr. Warner's Coraline Health Corsets. Their company, located in Bridgeport, Connecticut, employed over 1,000 seamstresses and produced 6,000 corsets a day. They offered free housing for female immigrants and classes in English and civics. Given those benefits, the company was not without controversy as the Warner Brothers Corset Company faced a strike of 1,300 women and girls organized as part of the International Textile Workers of America Union. In 1937, the Company went on to revolutionize brassiere design and manufacture by assigning letters to cup sizes. The company remains a powerhouse in the undergarment industry, including Olga brand, to this day.

Another eminent physician traveled back to New York in August. **Evarts Graham** identified himself as an "Author," rather than as the academic physician he was. On other voyages, he did state he was a doctor, and by 1955, he was "Retired"; two years later he died from lung cancer at age seventy-four. His career was remarkable in that by 1919, he had served two years as a Major in the United States Army Medical Corps, and revolutionized surgical techniques for the treatment of empyema, after the influenza pandemic of 1918. He commanded the United States Army Evacuation Hospital 34. Again in 1919, he was a full-time professor of surgery at the Washington School of

Medicine in St. Louis, Missouri, where he spent his career as a pulmonary surgeon. In 1933, he performed the first successful pneumonectomy, and in 1937 Graham helped found the American Board of Surgery.

A scant five years in the future, osteopath, **Dr. Albert Leon Sikkenga**, would lose his only son in Mageberg, Germany during World War II. Killed in action, **1st Lt. Albert L. Sikkenga, Jr.**, age twenty-four, piloted a bomber (751 Bomb SQ 457 Bomb GP) and was shot down. He is buried in Margraten, Netherlands, according to data from the American Air Museum in Britain. He was awarded a Purple Heart, Distinguished Flying Cross Air Medal with Four Oak Leaf Clusters. In 1935, the Sikkenga family lived in London and by 1939, the elder Sikkenga, in his early forties, was in private practice in Winter Park, Florida. While a student of osteopathy in Maine, he had registered for World War I, and he signed the *World War II Draft Registration Card 1942* (Old Man's Draft).

Pharmacologist **Marvin Russell Thompson** did not know it yet in 1939, but his research to eliminate dangerous reactions to sulfanilamide drugs would pay off in 1941, as reported in *Time Magazine* on April 21. On the trip in 1939, he traveled with his wife, **Florence** and their daughter **Dolores,** age eight. His credentials included PhD in Pharmacology and he worked at a private school in Great Neck, New York. He had lived in Washington, D. C. in 1930, working as a pharmacologist for the United States Government. He was, in fact, the Assistant Pharmacologist, Pharmacology Laboratory, Food, Drug and Insecticide Administration, U. S. Department of Agriculture. In 1930, he published his research in a series of articles for the *Journal of the American Pharmaceutical Association* in which he analyzed the use of ergot of rye, which was used to create medicines in Europe; ergot contains chemicals that help reduce bleeding.

Merchants

Charles M. Kennedy, who traveled with his family, indicated he was a "Politician" in 1939, but the *1940 US Census* states he was a grain merchant in New York, and employed at least one servant. He also may have been a politician, but the question asked for his occupation.

Joseph Sakin, born in 1904 in Lithuania, was an English national, a merchant and a "Hebrew" who resided in Shanghai, China, in 1939. On May 12, 1941, Sakin sailed aboard the *S. S. Mariposa Voy.* 59, a luxury cruise liner, from Honolulu to Los Angeles headed for England where he was married in either May or June. The history of the *S. S. Mariposa* mirrors that of many cruise ships during World War II; it became a fast troop carrier for five years and operated under the War Shipping Administration. So large, it was nicknamed a "monster" and usually sailed without an escort in the Pacific. In September 1942, it arrived in New York City with more than 100 American Volunteer

Group (Flying Tigers) pilots and ground personnel aboard. They had been denied transport back to the United States on half-empty transport planes by the U.S. Ferry Command. On April 15, 1943, the *Mariposa* carried military medical units and troops, including some Tuskegee Airmen, to Casablanca.

Leon F. Harris, fifty-two, traveled with his daughter, **Elizabeth**, eighteen, and resided in Highland Park, Illinois. He was sole proprietor of an Interior Decorating business, whose wife, **Ethel**, was his assistant.

There were several fur merchants aboard ship, including **August Friedrich Albers** and his wife **Carola**, traveling with their three-year old daughter, **Dorothee Carola**. They were berthed in Cabin Class and listed on the Quota Visa a list in addition to the full passenger list. He was born in Switzerland and she in Germany and were multi-lingual (as were many of the passengers) speaking German, French, and English. They settled in Seattle, Washington, and in 1940, August petitioned for naturalization stating clearly that he had arrived in the United States on August 11, 1939 aboard the *S. S. Nieuw Amsterdam*. He signed the petition on March 5, 1940, as an office manager, and in the *1940 US Census* he was a "Wholesale fur merchant," aged thirty-five, with five years of college education. On May 7, 1941, Carola stated she had come to the United States with her husband in 1939, under the name Carola Lili Albers, although her correct name was Lili Carola Albers. The fur industry thrived in the early 1900s, as French designers included wearing apparel such as fur trim, stoles, capes, or full fur coats for both women and men. There was a downturn in sales during the Depression and during World War II, but by the 1950s, fur sales increased.

Military Intelligence

Again I surmised this occupational category - "military intelligence." Likely, many of the well-educated, politically astute, and successful business people, as well as scientists on board the *S.S. Nieuw Amsterdam* were recruited into the war effort. I identified these three passengers as likely being heavily involved in the war.

Trevor Stamp, Jr. traveled Cabin Class with his mother, **Frances**, both Americans. His father, who became Lord Trevor Stamp in September 1941 because in April 1941 his parents and brother died in the Blitz, accompanied them. His name was on a separate list, indicating he was a British citizen. **Trevor Stamp**, born February 12, 1907, was a medical doctor and a bacteriologist who made many trips between Southampton and New York in the 1930s, principally to collaborate with scientists in the United States working on a program of biowarfare, according to *Britain and Biological Warfare: Expert Advice and Science Policy 1930-1965*. Working with scientists at Camp Detrick in Frederick, Maryland, and in Suffield, Ontario, and in Porton Down, England, he conducted open air tests, likely with anthrax. He received the American Medal of Freedom for his work on biological weapons. This type of research by the United

States and its allies in World War II continues to be widely discussed. Porton Down is home to two UK Government facilities and known for over one hundred years as one of the United Kingdom's most secretive and controversial military research facilities, occupying seven thousand acres.

Estel Burkhead Culbreth, Jr., born May 30, 1917, was in the U.S. Army, a second generation military veteran. He enlisted on June 12, 1939, and before his death, earned the rank of First Lieutenant. Why he was aboard the *S.S. Nieuw Amsterdam* in August 1939 is puzzling. Aunt Lucia did not mention seeing anyone in military uniform nor did she photograph anyone in uniform except the ship's Captain and some of the crewmembers. The *1940 US Census* listed his occupation as "government work." His death on August 27, 1941, is a mystery as he died stateside: "First Lt. Estel B. Culbreth, Jr., Infantry, August 27, 1941, at Richland, Georgia" according to the *US, Select Military Register, 1862-1985. Casualties, Active List. Army 1942. p. 972.*

In July 1918, the American Railway Express (ARE) was formed by the Federal government by consolidating four existing companies to safely and rapidly move packages, money, troops, and materiel to support the war effort. **Leonard Francis Whidden**, born November 13, 1875, had been a young married clerk in 1901, then a route agent for American Express in 1910, and was positioned perfectly to become the Chief Clerk for ARE when he signed his *World War I Draft Registration Card, 1917-1918*, on September 12, 1918. By 1940, Whidden was "General Agent, railway express" in Melrose City, Massachusetts. His position during both World Wars certainly provided essential support to the United States.

In 1936, Railway Express Agent, Leonard Francis Whidden (Whedden), applied for membership to the Massachusetts Society of the sons of the American Revolution. His paperwork described a clear line of descent from Henry Gates, a Minuteman serving during the Revolutionary War. Whidden signed the *World War II Draft Registration 1942*, still working for the Railway Express at the age of sixty-five.

Military Service

On this return trip, **Thomas Bailey Barrows,** born in 1892 in Philadelphia, was a business manager with four-years of college. He had served in World War I from June 30, 1918 to his discharge as a Private on November 5, 1919. During World War II he would be employed by the USO (United Service Organizations) on West Fortieth Street, New York, as he was too old to serve in the active military. He signed the *World War II Draft Registration Card* on April 26, 1942, just three months after the USO was headquartered in New York City.

Musicians

Among those who identified themselves as "Musicians" was **Edward Anthony Bonvalot**, a student in 1939, but then went on to create a career as a professional musician and composer. He followed in his famous father's footsteps: Captain Cecil Bonvalot, band director in the British military, was a member of the London String Quartet, a leading English chamber group into the 1930s.

On his *World War II Draft Registration Card*, **William John Bissett**, age thirty-four, stated he lived in Pima, Arizona, and worked as an orchestra leader at the Santa Rita Hotel, in Tucson. This was in October 1940, and he had been a musician at least since 1937. When he enlisted in the Army in 1943, Bissett had completed one year of college, was married, and was a teacher of music. Although he signed up for the duration of the war plus six months, he served only from January 11, 1943, to April 1, 1943. I could find no explanation.

Philanthropists

During World War I, the American YMCA was working with prisoners of war in Germany. **Conrad Hoffman, Jr., PhD**, fifty-five in 1939, had to complete complex paperwork to secure his position as "Secretary, YMCA" (actually, he was Senior Secretary) in this significant work in 1919. He was in his mid-thirties then when he served in England, France, and Germany between 1915 and 1919 (an American Protestant missionary) as indicated on his June 17, 1919, Passport Application, returning from France to the United States. The following statement was typed on the Application: "Identifying documents submitted as follows: letter from American YMCA requesting passport. Passport as above. Applicant is also bearer of a document issued by the Spanish Embassy in Berlin which enabled the applicant to leave Germany and enter France. Dean H. L. Russell University of Wisconsin, Madison, Wis; Dr. Jno R Mott, International Community YMCA, New York City." In cursive under this was: "Passport of Royal Spanish Embassy Attached."

Further, Hoffman had to complete the formidable form entitled *Affidavit to Explain Protracted Foreign Residence and to Overcome Presumption of Expatriation for Native and Naturalized Citizens* because he became an enemy alien living in Berlin when the United States declared war on Germany. He would need special permission to leave the country. Therefore, on the affidavit he stated: "I came abroad in 1915 as a YMCA Secretary in connection with the War Prisoner work. I remained in England for several months and then proceeded to Germany. I remained in Germany in this work up to two weeks ago. I had the approval of the Department of State in remaining in Germany." His passport was issued an "emergency passport" by the American Vice Consul.

Hoffman was not without company while he did this work on the War Prisoners Aid program. On at least three occasions – 1915, 1920, and 1922 – his wife **Louisa R. Hoffman** completed passport applications to accompany him to Europe on his YMCA service. Their two children were in Berlin with them from 1915 to 1917 and the YMCA officially appointed her to accompany him. The 1922 application indicated Louisa went to Switzerland to join her husband's work with the European Student Relief program.

The human service work done by the American YMCA had begun during the Civil War and preceded the work accomplished by the American Red Cross. During World War I, the YMCA performed ninety percent of the welfare work among soldiers in the American Expeditionary Forces. This effort included humanitarian services for five million or more prisoners of war in both Allied camps detaining enemy soldiers, and in Central Powers camps containing Allied troops. Readers may find substantial information online or in a long and detailed history, which contains President William Howard Taft's observation in a two-volume work titled *Service with Fighting Men: An Account of the Work of the American Young Men's Christian Associations in the World War* published in 1922. Hoffman wrote *In the Prison Camps in Germany*, which was published by Association Press in 1920. The work the YMCA accomplished was considerable, far reaching in humanitarian work, instrumental in the care of prisoners, and eventually replicated by branches of the United States military after World War II.

Politicians

Neil Oliver Staebler was born July 2, 1905, and identified himself as an "Artist" traveling with his wife, **Burnette,** in August 1939. Interestingly, the *1940 US Census*, states he was an "Executive, oil company" and he employed a maid. Again, the reasons for the subterfuge when asked to identify his occupation is puzzling in 1939. Staebler went on to serve on the staff of the Office of Price Administration and Civilian Supply from 1942-1943 – a source of policies and regulations on the rationing and pricing of oil, sugar, tires, cars, nylon, gasoline, fuel oil, coffee, meats, and processed foods during World War II. He served in the U.S. Navy from 1943-1945. Later he became a leader in the Democratic Party, eventually unsuccessfully challenging Republican Governor George Romney in the 1964 gubernatorial election. Staebler was a U.S. Representative At Large from Michigan, 1963-1965.

Philip Meyer Kaiser was born July 12, 1913, and in 1939, he traveled to New York with his wife, **Hannah**, stating he was a student. From 1936 to 1939, he studied at Balliol College, Oxford, as a Rhodes Scholar hence, naming himself as a "student" on the passenger list. He married in June, 1939, so it looks as though that trip may have been part of their honeymoon. The *1940 US Census* indicated both he and his wife had five years of college education, and he had been an economist for the Federal Reserve Board; in 1935 they lived in Madison, Wisconsin, likely attending the University of Wisconsin. His lifetime career was as Ambassador to Austria, Hungary, and Senegal and he served as Assistant Secretary of Labor for International Affairs in the Harry S. Truman administration. During the administration of President John F. Kennedy, Philip was named ambassador to Senegal and Mauritania, and later to Hungary under the Jimmy Carter administration. He retired from public service in 1981, but in 2000, he helped to pass a law that changed the name of the State Department headquarters to the Harry S. Truman building.

Professors

Robert Dudley French graduated from Yale University and went on to teach there from at least 1920 through World War II. He traveled to Europe during the 1920s for study and for pleasure.

Religious Leaders/Relief Workers

John Hassler Dietrich, born January 14, 1878, was a graduate of Franklin and Marshall College, traveled with his second wife **Margaret Carlton Winston Dietrich**, and was a minister for almost a quarter of a century at the First Unitarian Society in Minneapolis, Minnesota. He was among the first Unitarian ministers to boldly preach that humanist thinking was the true foundation of religious liberalism. His addresses, which were heard and read by thousands, so popularized religious humanism that it has now become a significant element in Unitarian Universalism. In 1942, Margaret, a writer and poet, published an account of her husband's life and thought, *This Circle of Earth*. A pioneer in the humanist movement, his papers are archived with the Minnesota Historical Society. Interestingly, he retired in 1938, but identified his occupation on this 1939 voyage as a "Lecturer," and she identified herself as a "Writer."

I found an enormous amount of information about **Dr. William Fletcher Quillian, Jr.**, born in 1913 in Georgia, and traveling back to the United States in Third Class. His father was President of Wesleyan College in Macon, and his father-in-law, Luther A. Weigle, was Dean of Yale Divinity School from 1928 to 1949. Weigle was also the Chair, Revised Standard Version Bible Committee of the National Council of Churches. Young Quillian was exceptionally well-educated: Emory University, Yale, and postgraduate studies at Edinburgh and the University of Basil. He married a Vassar graduate, and he was an ordained United Methodist minister. When he signed the *World War II*

Draft Registration Card in October 16, 1940, he stated he was a "Conscientious objector." He was twenty-seven years old and employed by Yale University. During the war he taught philosophy at Gettysburg College from 1941 to 1945. His life was devoted to dozens of philanthropic organizations and in 1952 he became President of Randolph Macon Women's College until his retirement in 1978.

I was irritated with this man and his claim to "CO" status when so many young people, including four of my aunt's brothers, headed off to war and Quillian stayed behind teaching philosophy. The definition of a CO is a person who claims the right to refuse to perform military service because of freedom of thought, or religion. During World War II, the draft law exempted from military service those who objected on the basis of religious training and belief. The COs were assigned to work of national importance such as serving as Army medics or, on the home front, served as forest fire fighters, attended the mentally ill, or completed conservation projects in rural areas. Quillian did none of these.

A second conscientious objector was **John Scott Everton,** born March 7, 1908, and was age thirty-two when he signed the *World War II Draft Registration Card* on October 16, 1940. He was a married minister at the Central Baptist Church in Wayne, Pennsylvania. He was educated at Colgate University, Cambridge and Yale. He was President of Kalamazoo College from 1949 to 1953, followed by a stint as an Ambassador to Burma from 1961 to 1963.

Scientists

John Wyatt Durham, born on August 22, 1907, was a geologist during World War II in the petroleum industry in Oakland, California. He is listed in *American Men and Women of Science, a Biographic Directory of Leaders in the Physical, Biological and Related Sciences 1971-1973*. In 1935 he lived on Kodiak Island and worked as a placer miner looking for mineral deposits – that is, gold and other minerals - in stream beds. During World War II, Fort Greeley was activated and was a base for the U.S. Coast Guard, U.S. Navy, U.S. Marines, U.S. Sea Bees, and the U.S. Merchant Marine.

Social Scientists

Dr. Hanns Sachs, born to a Jewish family in Vienna, Austria on January 10, 1881, cited Sigmund Freud as a mentor and friend. He was a lawyer who became enamored with Freud's work and began editing *Imago*, a journal devoted the non-medical applications of psychoanalysis. He moved to Boston in 1932 and became a naturalized American citizen on September 6, 1935, giving Berlin as his last foreign address, having emigrated from Havre,

France. He signed his *USA Declaration of Intent* as Dr. Hanns Sachs. He stated his occupation was "Author" when he traveled in 1939. He later wrote and published *Freud, Master and Friend* on June 1, 1944. Freud died in 1939. He went on to co-author *Masks of Love and Life: The Philosophical Basis of Psychoanalysis* with Abraham Aaron Roback and Anna Freud, and later he wrote *The Creative Unconscious: Studies in the Psychoanalysis of Art*, among other books in the field of psychoanalysis. The Hanns Sachs Library and Archives are part of the Boston Psychoanalytic Society and Institute devoted to the study of Sachs' work and that of other psychoanalyists.

A side note on this research gave me momentary pause: there was a second man on board with the same name, but different spelling, **Hans Sachs**, an antique dealer. Genealogical research can be heart-stopping, especially when one is taken down a side path!

Teachers

There were about sixteen people who identified their occupation as "Teacher" separate from those who used the term "Professor" (about three of these). **Leonide Marie Fleury** was forty-five on her return trip to Berkeley, California. Her specific job was puzzling as the *1940 US Census* data was sparse. She was listed as a "Bookkeepers assistant, student" and worked for a university. Her father, **Edward W. Flueury**, with whom she lived, worked for MacDonald & Kahn, Inc. in Pittsburgh, California, according to his *World War II Draft Registration Card 1942*, (Old Man's Draft). The company he worked for helped construct Oakland Army Base, Private Vehicle Inspection Building, on Africa Street and Bataan Avenue, Oakland. The initial construction began in 1942 and was used in support of Oakland Army Base's World War II mission.

Another Yale University graduate was **Theodore Culver Romney** a man who was part of Yale College's ROTC from 1916-1917. With five years of college education, he apparently spent his career teaching in a private school. At age forty-four, he enlisted in the U.S. Army, Branch Immaterial-Warrant Officers.

Writers

Henry W. Baude was born in Lithuania to Russian Jewish parents. He died about 90 days after signing the *U. S. World War II Draft Registration Cards, 1942* (Old Man's Draft) on April 25, 1942. He had also signed the *U.S. World War I Draft Registration Card, 1917-1918*, on June 5, 1917, verifying his place of birth/date of birth as February 22, 1888. In 1940, he was a lawyer in private practice in Cheltenham, Pennsylvania. Why he identified himself as a writer is unknown.

With a long career in newspaper journalism, **Lyndan Sluyter Dickie** worked for the News Syndicate Company, Inc., on E. 42nd Avenue, New York, during World War II. He signed the Old Man's Draft on April 25, 1942. During World War I, at the age of thirty-seven, Dickie worked for the New York American on Broadway. The *1925 New Jersey State Census* confirmed he had started his long career as a journalist in 1920 when he was the manager of a newspaper office in West Orange, New Jersey.

Women on board the August 1939 Voyage

Actresses

Katherine N. McGuirk attended Vassar in 1927 and traveled by ship many times. She was a secretary in a bank, but stated on this August 1939 voyage that she was an "Actress" born on December 29, 1907.

Edith Grater McCrea stated her occupation as "Singer" on this voyage. Born on September 1, 1902, she traveled extensively with her mother in the 1920s to Mexico, France, and Bermuda, and continued traveling after World War II. In 1930, she was employed as a teacher at a university and lodged with another family.

Another librarian, **Mary Fretageot** worked in a college in Saratoga Springs, New York in 1930, but became an "Actress" on her passage back to New York in August, 1939; she was thirty-four, born on November 21, 1905. She came from a long line of librarians: both her grandmother and an aunt shared her passion for books.

Gabrielle Kelen Stern was a "Quota Visa - Hebrew" born in 1908 in Vienna. On one list she identified herself as a "Housewife," but on the Quota Visa list, she identified herself as an "Actress."

Clerks/Stenographers

Rose Clare Floccher, born of Italian immigrants, was a thirty-nine year old stenographer "for the government" according to both the *1920* and *1930 US Census* for Washington, D. C. More specifically, she was a life-long employee of the Veterans Administration, starting as a typist and moving to analyst by 1948. In her career, she witnessed the 1921 creation of the Veterans Bureau, which consolidated all World War I veterans' programs through to a second consolidation in 1930 which created the Veterans Administration, a Federal agency. She apparently never married.

The Egan sisters traveled extensively by ship in 1929 and through the 1930s, primarily from New York City to England and Europe as found on the *New York, Passenger Lists, 1820-1957*. **Mary J. Egan**, born January 29, 1888, was the eldest, and **Marie E. Egan**, born May 15, 1894, and **Anita M. Egan**, born May 21, 1892, were the younger two. In 1920 Mary was a stenographer, Anita claimed no occupation, and Marie was a teacher in a public school. In 1920, they lived with their brother, John A. Egan, a civil engineer with New York City. Aboard ship, they listed their occupations as stenographer, "mannequin" (a person who models clothing), and teacher.

A secretary, **Stella C. Swede**, age thirty-five in 1939, was born in England, but worked as a clerk in the Stock Exchange, and lived with her sister in Brooklyn, New York. She was on the Quota Visa list for this voyage.

A student traveling home from England in 1939, **Janet Rhoda Jacobsohn**, nineteen, had been a student, but by 1940 was a salesperson of wholesale coats. Her father, Emmanuel Hezekial Jacobsohn, was a Russian Jew, born in Turkey before he immigrated to the United States, and was an importer of olive oil.

Fashion Designers

This category seemed to fit the lifelong work of **Edith Margaret Graf,** born in Vienna. She was registered on the Quota Immigrants Visa - Cabin Class, again, a second passenger list - as a thirty-five year old "Hebrew" who had no job. She was unmarried and remained so at least until she petitioned for naturalization through the U. S. District Court in Boston on January 29, 1945. She claimed entry to the United States as August 11, 1939, born in Austria, and she worked as a milliner. The witnesses on her petition were her landlady and another woman friend. In the *1940 US Census*, she was a lodger in Cambridge, Massachusetts, doing private hat making, and had a high school education.

Librarians

Giving her occupation as "Independent," **Helen M. Iredell** was born November 8, 1896, and was a college educated librarian working at a junior college in the 1930s. When she sailed to England in July 1939, she stated she was a "Librarian." Why the change in her stated occupation is unknown, since in 1940 she again identified herself as a librarian.

A single woman throughout her life, **Marcia A. Wheeler,** served as a librarian in a public library in Hinsdale, Illinois in 1940. She was age thirty-two. She had graduated from DePauw University in Greencastle, Indiana, in 1928, and was in the Kappa Alpha Omega Sorority. Her father, **Walton Mark Wheeler, Sr.**, was a successful lawyer in private practice, and employed servants in the household.

Medical Personnel

Dr. Dorothy Hewitt, born July 8, 1902, traveled with her partner, **Helen M. Iredel**, (see page 88). In 1930, Hewitt was an intern at Children's Hospital, San Francisco. In 1940, they lived in Long Beach, where Hewitt, a surgeon, had her own office.

Isabelle J. Holmen was a nurse at the age of twenty-five and returned to her home in Long Beach, California, in 1939. In 1940, she married mail carrier **David Booth Shepphird**, who served in the Army during World War II from 1942-1944. She retained her occupation as a nurse after marriage.

Military Service

In my last go-round in researching the passengers' names, I found **Frances L. Redhead**, born in 1915, and worked during the early 1940s in general office work in a cotton finishing plant. On January 28, 1943, she joined the U.S. Navy, and joined the Women's Auxiliary Volunteer Emergency Services. This organization was the precursor to Women Accepted for Volunteer Emergency Service. The WAVES was created in 1942 and its first commander was **Mildred Helen McAfee,** President of Wellesley College. By the end of the war, about 86,000 women served as WAVES (about 2% of the Navy). In 1948, Congress passed the Women's Armed Services Integration Act, creating them as a permanent fixture in the military. The WAVES was dissolved, but Redhead joined the Women's Reserve, U.S. Naval Reserve. Redhead was released from duty on January 25, 1961, after serving eighteen years. The Department of Veterans Affairs listed the date of death as August 13, 1972, at the age of fifty-seven.

No Occupation/Housewife

Initially, I skipped over the "housewives" but later in my research began to wonder just what means these women had at their disposal to afford multiple trips to Europe, sailing Cabin Class for the most part, from the early 1900s to 1939. That each of these women was labeled with a term no longer acceptable after about 1970, did not take away from the considerable social and cultural impact each made within her own social circles. With this in mind, the women took on a clearer role in my research.

Susan Worth Folger Oudin, widowed by 1930 at age sixty-five, and living on a pension, married **Maurice A. Oudin** in 1895. From 1900 through 1920 at least, Maurice was Vice President for the International General Electric

Company in New York and was an electrical engineer. Susan's passport application in 1893 identified her as the daughter of the United States Secretary of the Treasury, Charles James Folger, who was also a former Supreme Court Justice.

Their eldest child, **Charles Folger Oudin** received a Bachelor of Science Degree in electrical engineering in 1920 and was with the switch gear department of General Electric in Schenectady until 1932 when he retired. During World War II, he served as chairman of the Otsego County Office of Price Administration and Civilian Supply, an office created to control rents and the overall cost of items that might be affected by the war (as per Executive Order 8875 on August 28, 1941); it was responsible for rationing programs nationwide.

Although she had five plus years college education, on this trip **Mary Christine Drach**, age forty, was listed simply as a "Housewife." Her husband, **Harvey Edward Drach**, born in 1897, was a professor at the University of Cincinnati.

Mother and daughter traveled together in 1939; **Esther J. Woodings,** age sixty-two, sailed with **Marjorie Woodings**, age twenty-four. The Woodings household was well-to-do according to the *1930 US Census*, the household was worth $45,000 and the family had three children and employed one servant from at least 1910. **Emanuel Robert Woodings** moved in his career from machinist to superintendent to owner of the Woodings-Verona Tool Works, Verona, Pennsylvania, founded in 1883 to manufacture a variety of tools used to maintain iron and steel production and to support the mining industry. Esther and her daughter were well able to travel extensively.

By 1940 the company was called the Emmanuel Tool Manufacturing, with son **Wilbert Henry Woodings** working as a salesman. By 1949 it became Woodings Industrial, the oldest continuous family-operated business in the steel industry in North America, and is an international leader in the design, manufacture, and service of taphole drills, clayguns, and for other products that are integral to the metals industry.

Similarly, **Emma A. Wuffling Bower** was in her fifties, when she and her daughter, **Barbara Ann Bower,** fourteen, traveled from England. Well-traveled, the family afforded these trips because Emma's husband, **Joseph A. Bower**, was the Vice President of a bank in Montclair, New Jersey. The family employed a cook and a butler in 1940.

I could not find data on **John Goodenday**, a "Hebrew" company director, whose success allowed him and his wife, **Eileen Mary Ruth Goodenday,** to travel extensively Cabin Class from the 1930s through 1960. His career path took him from company director to chairman, but I was unable to determine the nature of his business. I was unable to find information on his daughter or his son, so the elder Goodenday's life remains a history mystery.

Philanthropists

Many women associated themselves with philanthropic organizations, which may have been voluntary, but often positively impacted the lives of those around them. **Florence Wardwell** was no exception in her work with the American Relief Administration in 1920. The ARA, formed in 1919, had future President Herbert Hoover as its program director, and he oversaw the delivery of tons of relief supplies to twenty-three countries. What Florence's role was is not specified. Apparently she never married, traveled extensively to England in the early 1900s and the 1930s, always during the summer. Her father was **Henry Lansing Wardwell**, a stock broker and senior partner of Wardwell & Adams, and a member of the New York Stock Exchange. Since no occupation could be discerned, presumably she inherited money from her parents.

Professors

Clearly from the upper classes, **Margaret Louise Fincke**, born October 24, 1900, to a physician from Scotland, lived in New York and toured Europe when she was a twenty-two year old student. She went to Italy, the British Isles, France, Holland, Germany, Belgium, and Austria aboard the *Metagama*, leaving New York on June 3, 1922. Parenthetically, this ship had served as a troop transport ship during World War I, and was built for the Canadian Pacific Railroad Company.

In 1930 Margaret's occupation was "Chemist, college." On the return voyage to New York in 1939, she declared her occupation as an "Artist"; she was age thirty-eight. In 1940, she was employed as a "Professor of foods and nutrition" at Oregon State College. She went on to co-author *Station Technical Bulletin 12 (December 1943): A Study of Ascorbic Acid Metabolism of Adolescent Children,* as part of her role at the School of Home Economics, at Oregon State College. She had been conducting ascorbic acid research at least since 1942 and published in the *Journal of Nutrition and the Journal of Food Science.* She became Professor and Head of the Department of Foods and Nutrition, Oregon State College. Since she was from Corvalis, it is likely she knew or knew of the Whiteside family whose theater business is mentioned on page 76.

Born in Mexico City in 1903 to **Charles Stanley, Rosamond Elizabeth Beatrice Stanley** became a naturalized American citizen in 1913. In the 1930s she traveled to the United Kingdom as a professor. She did not marry until 1941, then to **Jaime Vidal Colome**.

Ann Elizabeth Mensel was a British citizen born in 1886 in Iver, England, and by 1939 identified herself as

"Professor." On other voyages (1937 and 1948), she used the term "Teacher." Significantly, when she traveled with her husband, **Ernst Heinrich Mensel**, who from 1920 was a Professor of Germanic Languages at Smith College, she was again a "Teacher." They traveled First Class. Widowed in 1942, she again used the term "Professor" and used it throughout the rest of her life. A call to Smith College librarian confirmed that Ann was employed by the college and she taught German.

Born in Christchurch, New Zealand, **Elizabeth Neige Todhunter**, age thirty-eight returned to her teaching job in Pullman, Washington, in 1939. This was corroborated by the information on her U. S. Naturalization Papers, signed on December 21, 1939. She had received her PhD in Nutrition from Columbia University in 1933 and went on to teach Home Economics at the State College of Washington from 1934-1941. She moved to the University of Alabama, initially as Director of the Research Laboratory of Human Nutrition from 1941-1953, then as Professor and Dean, Department of Food and Nutrition from 1953-1966. She was also President of the American Dietetic Association from 1957-1958.

In 1966, when she retired, she was Visiting Professor of Nutrition in the Department of Biochemistry at Vanderbilt University School of Medicine from 1967-1991, Nashville, Tennessee. She developed the Annette and Irwin Eskind Biomedical Library Special Collections History of Nutrition Collection. I wonder if she liked the food aboard the *S.S. Nieuw Amsterdam* as much as my Aunt Lucia did.

Religious Leaders/Relief Workers

I could not determine if **Elizabeth Dewart**, born July 11, 1917, was traveling alone back to her home in Massachusetts from England. She gave her occupation, at age twenty-two, as "None." She was, in fact, one of seven children born to **William Herbert Dewart**, Episcopal Rector at Christ Church in Boston from 1914 to 1927 (Herringshaw's *American Blue Book of Biography*). The family home was in the posh Back Bay area of Boston, and they listed seven servants as seen in the *1920 US Census*. The fame of this historic church, established in 1722, is steeped in the history of the U.S. Revolutionary War. The Old North Church is where two lanterns were hung as a signal from Paul Revere that the British were traveling up the Charles River to Cambridge to march on Lexington. The church was closed from April 1775 to August 1778 during the Revolutionary War.

Freda Millicent Yates, born July 29, 1913, was a nurse in 1939 and presumably put her skills to use as the wife of **Stephen Yates**, a missionary stationed in Papua New Guinea for at least two decades. The long involvement of Christian missionaries in Papua New Guinea goes back to the mid-1800s.

A co-religionist aboard the ship was **Julia Nestle Drew,** a woman in her late seventies, and recently a widow of the **Reverend Edward Payson Drew,** former Pastor of the Congregational Church in Newton, Massachusetts. He had died in April 1935. In 1930, he was a professor at Andover Theological School serving as both professor and Director of Graduate Work from at least 1929 through 1933. Prior to this, he went to China in 1916 to teach. Interestingly, he and Julia traveled in 1917 to Japan (which had joined the Allies) and to England in 1918, and again in 1924. Travel by sea during World War I (July 1914 to November 1918) was treacherous as Allied merchant ships were attacked by Germany, and Britain mined international waters, making the way dangerous for neutral ships. Further, in 1917, Germany launched unrestricted submarine warfare.

Scientists

Of particular note was the occupation of **Dr. Muriel Robertson**, born in Scotland on April 8, 1883, who identified herself as a "Scientist" and on the *Visitor to the United States* list, as "Scientific Researcher." Researching the National Library of Scotland yielded the story of an amazing woman who was chiefly recognized for her research on parasites which cause illnesses such as sleeping sickness. During both world wars, she made significant strides in treating gangrene. She received her Doctor of Science in 1923 at the age of forty and was a proto-zoologist and bacteriologist from 1915 to 1961. After World War II, she was elected as a Fellow of the Royal Society in 1947. Robertson was one of the first women elected to this prestigious society.

Writers

M. Elizabeth Yates was the author of the 1951 children's book *Amos Fortune, Free Man*. The book was based on the life of a freed slave in New England and it won the 1951 Newberry Medal for Children's Literature and was translated into several languages. Well educated, Yates received seven honorary degrees and other literary awards. She wrote an autobiographical trilogy and biographies of some strong-willed people. One was *Prudence Crandall*, published in 1955, about a teacher who defied Connecticut law in 1833 when she opened a private girls' school that accepted black and white pupils as equals. Yates traveled with her husband, **William Jones McGreal,** discussed earlier on page 74. At her death in 2001, Yates had authored over fifty books, many of them for children.

ENDING THE RESEARCH

I did not research every single person who sailed with my Aunt on these summer voyages. However, I think I have painted a picture of the disparity in the lives of very privileged tourists versus the working class of the time. Hopefully, I did this without a heavy moral hand. Events leading to war, war itself, and the aftermath of war changes everyone. This is life.

The conclusion of research is what writers strive for, I think, even though the end may leave the writer searching for another topic, or another ancestor (perhaps another aunt?). As many anthropologists, historians, biographers, and genealogists know, research can be many things at once: happy, focused, exciting, sloppy, frustrating, and a serendipitous adventure looking into the lives of one's own ancestors, or into the lives of people to whom one is not even remotely related. It's all the same process and one that I relish. In the months it took me to research and to write, my Saturdays and vacation days were consumed with trips to the Latter-Day Saints Family History Center, or virtual trips to the Duluth Public Library, or phone calls to more experienced historians, genealogists, or librarians. I truly enjoyed the research and the writing, and hope that my readers will be inspired to hang some clothes on their own family tree.

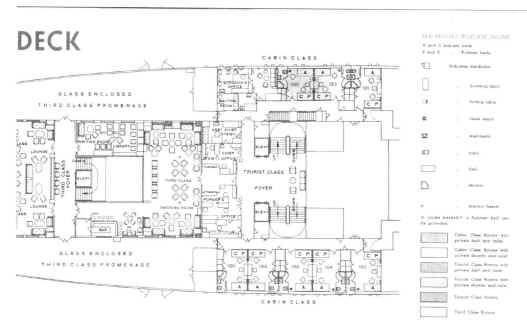

Notes on Citing My Sources

My background is steeped in academia, so it seemed correct for me to cite my sources for every fact in painful detail. I decided not to be strictly academic in doing so because I thought it took away from telling the story. I have no plans to submit the book for peer review; the story of my aunt, a young woman on an adventure trip does not warrant that step.

With these things in mind, my readers should know that I triangulated data by using the following resources, both on-line and hardcopy:

General Genealogical Resources

Ancestry.com

FindaGrave.com

FindmyPast.com

Fold3

Obituaries

State Military Service Records

U. S. College and University Yearbooks

United States Official Documents On-Line

U. S. Census 1900-1940

U. S. State Census 1905-1925

Census Publications (www.census.gov/library/publications)

1939 US City Directory 1821-1989 (Minneapolis and other cities)

U. S. Passport Applications (Ancestry.com)

U. S. Naturalization Applications (Ancestry.com)

U. S. World War I Draft Registration Cards, 1917-1918 (Ancestry.com or Fold3)

U. S. World War II Draft Registration Cards (Ancestry.com or Fold3)

U. S. World War II Registration Cards (Old Man's Draft) (Ancestry.com or Fold3)

U. S. Select Military Register, 1862-1985 Casualties, Active List. Army. 1942 - (https://search.ancestry.com)

Minnesota Public Radio - (https://www.mprnews.org Documentary: No Jews Allowed)

U. S. Department of Labor, 1936 Edition, Handbook of Labor Statistics. - (https://fraser.stlouisfed.org)

U. S. Department of Labor, Women in the Economy of the United States of America: A Summary Report (https://fraser.stlouisfed.org)

United States General Resources On-Line

Rockefeller Foundation Digital History - (https://rockfound.rockarch.org/biographical)

Woodings Industrial Corporation - (http://www.woodingsindustrial.com)

Institute for Advanced Study - (https://www.ias.edu)

American Air Museum in Britain - (http://www.americanairmuseum.com)

United States Railroad History

Railroaders Memorial Museum - (www.railroadcity.com)

United Kingdom Official Documents On-Line

1911 Census (England and Wales)

1939 Register (England) - (www.findmypast.co.uk/1939register/what-is-the-1939-register)

National Archives (England) - (www.nationalarchives.gov.uk)

Historical Newspapers (England) - (www.newspapers.com/place-county-england)

National Library of Scotland - (https://www.nls.uk)

United Kingdom General Resources On-Line

Weather History - (london-weather.eu/article.80.html)

History Wilshire County - (history.wiltshire.gov.uk)

History Somerset County - (www.wellssomerset.com)

William Shakespeare - (theshakespeareblog.com/2014/02/Judith-quiney-shakespears-forgotten-daughter)

War in England On-Line

Aviation History (England; search by airport, timeframe, location)

Naval History - (http://naval-history.net/WW2CampaignsUboats.htm)

History of War – Lockheed Aircraft - (www.historyofwar.org/Lockeed)

Home Guard - (wikipedia.org/wiki/Home_Guard)

Anderson Shelters - (primaryfacts.com/506/anderson-shelter-facts/)

World War II Air Campaign: Air Raid Precautions - (histclo.com/essay/war/ww2/air/eur/bob/arp/arp.html)

Bristol Blitz - (en.wikipedia.org/wiki/Bristol_Blitz)

Bristol Aviation History - (www.aviation-history.com/bristol/beaufite.html)

Bristol Aviation History - (en.wikipedia.org/wiki/Bristol_Aeroplane_Company#Second_World_War)

War in the Pacific

Tatsuta Maru/World War II Database - (https://ww2db.com/ship)

On-Line General

Spirella Corset Company - (https://en.wikisource.org/wiki/Spirella_Corsets 1913)

History of Potato Chips - (wow.todayifoundout)

History of Whiteside Theater - (http://whitesidetheater.org and www.corvalisadvocate.com)

Maritime and Airline Passenger Manifests

UK, Incoming Passenger Lists, 1878-1960 "Names and Description of ALIEN Passengers"

UK, Outward Passenger Lists, 1890-1960 "Names and Descriptions of ALIEN Passenger"

New York Passenger Lists 1820-1953, microfilm, 1943, US Department of Justice

List or Manifest of Aliens Employed on the Vessel - *SS Nieuw Amsterdam*

Cruise Line History

Cruising the Past - (http://cruiselinehistory.com/1930s)

Classic Liners of Yesteryear - (www.ssmaritime.com)

Holland America Lines

Holland America Blog - (www.hollandamericablog.com)

Historical Brochures - (www.gjenvik.com/HistoricalBrochures/UnitedStatesLines/1938)

Holland America Blog - (www.hollandamericablog.com/captains-from-the-past/filipo-abraham/)

War History/History of War

War History on Line - (www.warhistoryonline.com)

Military History - (www.militaryhistoryonline.com)

World War II Database - (https://ww2db.com)

Farsleben - (www.30thinfantry.org/farsleben)

Hardcopy Resources

St. Michael's Church, Dundry, Burials 1658-1887 (handwritten document/CD).

RECOMMENDED READING

Clayton, Meg Waite. 2015. *The Race for Paris*. New York: Harper Collins Publishers.

Duenas, Maria. 2009. *The Time in Between*. Madrid: Ediciones Planeta. Daniel Hahn. 2011. English translation. New York: Atria Books (Simon and Schuster, Inc.)

Garrett, Patrick. 2015. *Of Fortunes and War: Clare Hollingsworth, first of the female war correspondents*. London: Thistle Publishing.

Joukowsky, Artemis. 2016. *Defying the Nazis: The Sharps' War*. Boston: Beacon Press.

Metaxas, Eric. 2010. *Bonhoeffer: Pastor, Martyr, Prophet, Spy – A Righteous Gentile vs The Third Reich*. Nashville: Thomas Nelson.

Mulley, Clare. 2012. *The Spy Who Loved: The Secrets and Lives of Christine Granville*. New York: St. Martin's Press.

Mundy, Liza. 2017. *Code Girls: The Untold Story of the American Women Code Breakers of World War II*. New York: Hachette Books.

Ottaway, Susan. 2013. *A Cool and Lonely Courage: The Untold Story of Sister Spies in Occupied France*. New York: Little, Brown and Company.

Paillole, Paul. 2016. *The Spy in Hitler's Inner Circle: Hans-Thilo Schmidt and the Intelligence Network that Decoded Enigma*. Oxford & Philadelphia: Casemate.

Porter, Carolyn. 2017. *Marcel's Letters: A Font and the Search for One Man's Fate*. New York: Skyhorse Publishing.

Quinn, Kate. 2017. *The Alice Network*. New York: Harper Collins Publishers.

Rigg, Bryan Mark. 2016. *The Rabbi Saved by Hitler's Soldiers: Rebbe Joseph Isaac Schneersohn and His Astonishing Rescue*. Lawrence, Kansas: University Press of Kansas.

Rosen, Robert N. 2000. *The Jewish Confederates*. Columbia, South Carolina: University of South Carolina Press.

Sebba, Anne. 2016. *Les Parisiennes: How the Women of Paris Lived, Loved and Died Under Nazi Occupation*. New York: St. Martin's Press.

Stevenson, William. 2007. *Spymistress: The Life of Vera Atkins, the Greatest Female Secret Agent of World War II*. New York: Arcade Publishing.

ACKNOWLEDGEMENTS

Thanks to Marlene Wisuri, Dovetailed Press, Duluth, Minnesota, for her keen eye and excellent editing which helped me keep the story accurate as well as interesting. Her experience as a genealogist and historian were invaluable. Thanks to First Photo, Duluth, Minnesota, that expertly scanned the scrapbook photos for use in this story.

The volunteer genealogists at the Family History Center, Church of Jesus Christ of Latter-Day Saints, Duluth, provided expert guidance and access to the institutional versions of Ancestry and many other websites so vital to this research. I most appreciate their unfailing willingness to assist me in all phases of this research.

Thank you to Ken Buehler, Executive Director, Lake Superior Railroad Museum, Duluth, Minnesota, who provided valuable information about train travel in 1939 from Minneapolis to New York.

Reuben Goossens, webmaster of S. S. Maritime, provided in-depth data about luxury cruise liners that served as troop transports during World War II in both the Atlantic and Pacific Theaters.

My thanks to my cousins for their assistance in creating this snapshot in time. Carol Payton Spaulding provided our Aunt Lucia's letters, photo albums and school scrapbooks which are the foundation for the story. Cousin Jane Day Hamblin, Dundry, England, contributed valuable information about Payton family life during World War II and has consistently encouraged the writing. Cousin Countess Annabelle de la Panouse provided interesting stories about our Aunt Lucia and enthusiastically read the initial draft of the book. And thanks to five other cousins for their encouragement and pieces of information about Aunt Lucia: Genie Jensen, Katie Jensen, Ruth Hollister, Jane Seesz, and Richard Gee.

And my thanks to the Reference Librarian at the New York Historical Society, as well as to volunteers who answered my questions at The Telecommunications History Group, Inc., in Denver, Colorado, and at the Altoona Railroad Museum in Altoona, Pennsylvania. Thanks to Richmond Kinney, Technical Services, Duluth Public Library, in Duluth, Minnesota. Thanks to Claire Twinn, Hong Kong and Shanghai Bank Senior Archives Manager, and to her assistant, Matilda B. J. Knowler, for answering questions about that corporation's employees during World War II. Marie Concannon, Head, Government Information and Data Archive, Ellis Library, University of Missouri,

Columbia, provided valuable resources on labor statistics from the 1930s through the 1940s, and information on the unionizing of American communications workers.

I especially thank R. Michael Busch, my husband, who provided text and photo technical assistance to illustrate the document. Additionally, I learned from Mike, who lived in Holland in 1959-1961, that the Dutch breakfasts always served "Holland rusks." It is a round bread about one inch thick, very crisply toasted and served hot or cold, but usually cold. Typically, they are served with cheese, marmalade or jam for a choice of toppings. These may have been what Aunt Lucia described.

And to my friend, Cora Knutson, who provided guidance whenever my formatting went "wonky" or when the Internet chose to go down. Thank you to Marcia Runnberg-Valadez, who read and commented on an early draft with an eye to movie rights for the story! It takes a village.

By that time the entire room was roaring

Someone just called me to see the sun go down it was beautiful like a huge ball of fire just dropping in the ocean, it is twenty minutes after nine + still light enough to read.

Sunday Morning –

Won another prize last night + believe it or not I won the prize dancing I still can't believe it – must have been a put up job, Every one is pointing me out as the lucky one.

Drank my first sherry too + I wed Ruis again I didn't loose any money though because my american friend insisted on paying for my cards, so I think, "OK sap"–

Got to bed at four a.m. + slept until twelve but Sunday is the same as any other day on ship, except for our church this morning, I did miss the Tribune though this is a very little thing when I think how much I wish you were all here.

ABOUT THE AUTHOR

Kathleen M. Cargill is a cultural anthropologist who received her Bachelor's Degree at the University of Michigan, Ann Arbor. She completed her Master's Degree in Anthropology as well as doctoral research and dissertation at the University of Florida, Gainesville. She used genealogy as part of her graduate anthropology research including the study of the adequacy of slave nutrition, the study of a rural Florida migrant health clinic, and the study of a rural Florida fire department. These experiences allowed her to move into her own family genealogy after her retirement as an adjunct teacher at The College of St. Scholastica, Duluth, Minnesota, and as that college's first Director of the Ronald E. McNair Scholars Program. Kathleen is a member of the Minnesota Historical Society, the Minnesota Genealogical Society, the Twin Ports Genealogical Society, the Archaeological Conservancy, and the Wayzata Historical Society. In addition to Kathleen's passion for anthropology, genealogy, and history, she is an avid gardener and sole owner of Beekeeper's Press.

Photo by Mike Busch

HOLLAND-AMERICA
LINE

NIEUW AMSTERDAM